Die drei ???®

Die drei ???®
Evil Games

von André Marx

Aus dem Deutschen ins amerikanische Englisch übertragen von Chris und Tracey Huber

Kosmos

Umschlagillustration von Silvia Christoph, Berlin
Umschlaggestaltung von eStudio Calamar, Girona, auf der Grundlage der Gestaltung von Aiga Rasch (9.Juli 1941–24.Dezember 2009), Leinfelden-Echterdingen

FSC www.fsc.org
MIX
Papier aus verantwortungsvollen Quellen
FSC® C014138

Gedruckt auf chlorfrei gebleichtem Papier

ISBN 978-3-440-12332-4

Die deutsche Originalausgabe erschien unter dem Titel „Die drei ??? ® Spur ins Nichts“ bei Franckh-Kosmos Verlags-GmbH & Co KG. (ISBN 978-3-440-10209-2)
Mit freundlicher Genehmigung der Universität von Michigan

Based on characters by Robert Arthur.

Übersetzung: Chris und Tracey Huber
Bearbeitung: Katja Demuth
Redaktion: Ina Brandt
Produktion: DOPPELPUNKT, Stuttgart
Printed in the Czech Republik / Imprimé en République tchèque

Die drei ???®

Evil Games

Awakening

It was dark.
It was cold.
Something was aching. His bones? His head? Something.
Justus Jonas was waking up more slowly than he ever had before in his life. Minute by minute, as **consciousness** slowly dawned on him, he touched his own body as if it didn't belong to him and with great **effort** shook off the **fuzzy** dreams.
Dreams … There was a warehouse. A spotlight. A brown island in a white sea. A young man with light blond hair. An important **message** on a piece of paper. A hiding place … But with every passing second the **memory** continued **fading**. And when Justus finally opened his eyes, the dream was as good as forgotten.
It was still dark. What time might it be? A look at the alarm clock …
There was no alarm clock. No night stand on which it could have been sitting. There was not even a bed. Justus was lying on the smooth, hard ground. That's why everything ached. That's why he was freezing. He sat up. He couldn't even see his own hand in front of his face. Where was he?
It took a while, but then the question resulted in such a sheer adrenaline rush that Justus was catapulted completely out of sleep. This was not his room!
Light! He needed light! Justus pushed himself up and rose

---

consciousness – Bewusstsein; **effort** – Anstrengung;
fuzzy – verschwommen; **message** – Nachricht;
memory – Erinnerung; **to fade** – verblassen

slowly onto **wobbly** feet. He felt a cold **tile wall**. Cautiously Justus took a step forward. Then a step farther, keeping the wall at his side. There had to be a door here somewhere! Or at least a light switch! Fear gripped Justus like an icy hand. Something was completely amiss here. Reality had **come apart at the seams**. And he had no idea why. He broke out in a sweat. He needed light at long last!
There! His fingers felt something square. He pressed it. It flashed. It flashed again. And then bright, cold fluorescent light flickered on with an electric hum.
It blinded Justus so much so that he put his hand over his eyes. Carefully, he ventured a second **glance**. Gradually his eyes became accustomed to the brightness. But what he saw did not **reassure** him at all. On the contrary.
The room looked like a former operating room. It was windowless and had white tiles up to the ceiling. The tiles were dirty, here and there were dark outlines from things that had once stood or hung there. Below the ceiling two fluorescent tubes were mounted, there was a gray door on a wall. Otherwise the room was empty. Empty except for a dark ball on the floor in the corner.
Justus jumped. Someone was lying there! And this someone was just waking up. Justus rushed to him, a young man in his early twenties with tousled black hair and equally black eyes. He blinked confusedly toward the fluorescent lights.
When he noticed Justus, he was **startled**.

---

wobbly – wackelig; **tile wall** – gekachelte Wand;
to come apart at the seams – aus den Fugen geraten; **glance** – Blick;
to reassure – beruhigen; **to be startled** – erschrocken sein

"Hello," Justus said quickly. "Don't be frightened. I'm … uh … completely harmless."
It took a moment for the young man to **get his bearings** and to sit up. He pressed himself into the corner and took up a defensive posture. "Who are you?" he asked with a **hoarse voice**.
"My name is Justus Jonas. I just woke up myself and just turned on the light."
The man looked at Justus as if he had **lost his marbles**. Justus could not blame him. He wasn't completely certain regarding his own mental state. "We'd better leave this unpleasant place right away," he suggested, in order to say something constructive.
The man didn't react.
Justus went to the door and turned the handle. **Locked**. "Well, it's going … less optimally than I had hoped."
"What kind of a **crackpot** are you?" The stranger asked **threateningly**.
"I am not a crackpot. Like I already said, my name is Justus Jonas, and – "
"Did you lock us in here?"
"Locked in? No! I … I have no idea who … "
"Where are we?"
"I don't know."

---

to get one's bearings – zu sich kommen;
hoarse voice – raue Stimme;
to lose one's marbles – nicht mehr alle Tassen im Schrank haben;
locked – verschlossen;
crackpot – Spinner;
threateningly – bedrohlich

"I'm warning you, you freak!" threatened the guy across from him. "**Don't give me any crap**! How did you get here?"
"I …" began Justus and swallowed hard. "I don't know. And unfortunately that's not crap but the truth. I don't have the faintest idea how I got here or where we are. I can't remember anything."

The snow was blindingly bright and enveloped the mountains in gorgeous white. The wind was icy and swept the heat out of his body. Peter looked down at himself. He was wearing cut-off jeans and a thin T-shirt. No wonder he was freezing. What had he been thinking going on a ski vacation in these clothes? His girlfriend Kelly, who stood next to him, was laughing at him. Why not? She had thought of everything, in fact, and stood before him in a warm and cozy-looking pink ski suit, her eyes protected from the light by dark ski goggles. She heartily bit into something that smelled strongly of fish. A fish burger?

Suddenly she grabbed him by the shoulders and **shook** him. What was she doing that for? Did she somehow think that would warm him up? "Hey," shouted Kelly and shook him further. "Hey you! Hey! Heeey!"
"What are you doing?" protested Peter. "What are you doing?"
The shaking became more violent. "Now wake up already!"
Wake up? What on earth did she mean by wake up? He was standing wide awake in front of her! Or maybe not? Or was it possible perhaps that he was dreaming? Was that the reason why he was in shorts of all things in the snow … "Hey!"

---

don't give me any crap – erzähl mir keinen Mist; **to shake** – schütteln

Peter woke up. "All right, all right," he muttered. "I'm awake." He opened his eyes. It was still glisteningly bright around him. And the cold had also not **disappeared**. So really not a dream? He looked down at himself. Cut-off jeans and a thin T-shirt. At least that part of the dream was real. Peter turned his head. There was actually a girl who sat beside him and had shaken him awake. But it wasn't Kelly. The girl had brown, wild **curls** and **freckles** and was wearing jeans and a white hoodie. Peter had never seen her before.

"What … what happened?"

"I wish I knew. Finally you're awake! I thought you were in a coma or something!"

"Coma? I … " Peter **trailed off**. Darn it, he wasn't able to think straight at all. So, he had been dreaming, all right. Nevertheless, it was white around him and it was cold. And it still smelled of fish, although there were no fish burgers to be seen. And there was a **strange** girl who was **bending over** him. White? Coma? Girl? Maybe he was in a hospital. But why did it stink so horribly here then?

"Did I have an accident?"

"What? No. That is, I don't know." The girl was visibly nervous. "I don't even know who you are."

"Peter," said Peter. "Peter Shaw. Where am I?"

"You … you don't know?" She looked at him with her big brown eyes. Then she slid a bit to the side to allow a clear view of the room.

Peter sat up irritated. What he saw reminded him of an ope-

---

to disappear – verschwinden; **curls** – Locken;
freckles – Sommersprossen; **to trail off** – abbrechen;
strange – fremd, komisch; **to bend over** – sich beugen über

rating room in a hospital. However, it was not particularly clean. And the equipment consisted of only some fluorescent lights beneath the ceiling which were producing the blindingly bright light. There was a door. No windows.

"Do you remember it again?" the girl asked hopefully.

"Remember it? No. I've never been here. How did I get here?"

"Are you even listening to me at all? I – do – not – know. I woke up here fifteen minutes ago and don't have the **slightest clue** where we are. I was hoping *you* could tell me that!"

"I? Why … " Peter trailed off. He tried to remember. Why was he here? How did he get here? But his **mind** was completely **blank**. What had happened before sleeping … was gone. He did not even have a clue what day it was. Peter glanced at his digital watch. Saturday, the fourth of October. 3:12 pm. OK, slowly now. He felt as if he had slept all night. What had yesterday been then? Yesterday, on Friday? What had he done? Where had he been? With whom? Why?

"Hello!" cried the girl half angry, half **anxious** and waved her hand around in front of his face. "Are you still there? Are you OK?"

Another question that Peter could hardly answer. Was he well? How did he feel? He had absolutely no idea. He felt somehow … nothing at all. Only his stomach was not feeling particularly good. It was empty. And the intense smell of fish was getting to him. Nevertheless, he said: "Yes, everything's great. I think. Tell me, who are you anyway?"

"Jolene Sprague."

---

slightest clue – geringster Hinweis; **mind** – Verstand, (hier) Kopf; **blank** – leer; **anxious** – ängstlich

"And you yourself just –"
"Woke up, yes. And I have no idea where we are. What … what's going on? Have we been kidnapped? By whom? What do they want from us? I … " Jolene broke off. Breathed deeply. And continued in a **trembling** voice: "You must know something!"
"But, I don't know anything!" Peter retorted more harshly than he had wanted. "I … I have to come to my senses, do you understand? Wake up. Clear my head."
Jolene looked at him as if he had suggested playing a round of cards. She stood up and **paced desperately back and forth** in the room. Finally she stopped at the gray door and kicked it. "Crap!"
"The door is probably –"
"Locked, exactly," Jolene interrupted him. "I tried a hundred times earlier to get it open."
"Jolene," began Peter, and slowly rose to his feet, "I'm not sure if I just understood everything correctly, but … can you remember anything that's **related to** this place? Or with how you came to be here? I'm quite obviously having … problems with my memory."
Jolene stopped and looked at him bewildered. "Then you're not the only one."
"You mean –"
"That I also don't remember anything either? That's exactly what it means."

---

trembling – zitternd;
to pace desperately back and forth – verzweifelt auf- und ablaufen;
to be related to – zusammenhängen mit

Cries for Help

Shawn, which was the young man's name as Justus had found out in the meantime, had calmed down a bit. Still he stared at Justus **gloomily** from his coal-black eyes, but at least he no longer gave the **impression** that he wanted to **strangle** him at any moment.

Both paced restlessly back and forth in the room. Justus was **deep in thought** which seemed to make Shawn nervous.

"Why are you constantly pulling on your bottom lip?" he snapped at him. "It's driving me crazy!"

"I'm thinking," muttered Justus.

"Oh! What do you think I'm doing? I'm thinking too! I'm thinking about how we're getting out of here!"

"I'm more **preoccupied with** the question of how we got in here. What are your last memories?"

"Memories? Of what?"

"In general. What is the last thing you remember?"

Shawn stood still for a moment. "I was in a new club in L. A. Last night. And then … " He frowned. "I don't know. Somehow **I've blacked out**."

"Did you drink alcohol?"

"Maybe so. I don't know. Not much anyway, I drove there."

---

gloomily – finster, bedrohlich;
impression – Eindruck;
to strangle – erwürgen;
to be deep in thought – tief in Gedanken versunken sein;
to be preoccupied with – sich beschäftigen mit;
I've blacked out – Ich habe einen Filmriss

"So, it seems that high alcohol consumption is not the reason for your **amnesia**," determined Justus.
"What? Hey, why are you talking like that?"
Justus blushed slightly. "Sorry. I ... speak like that sometimes. I can't help it. Shawn, are you sure that your visit to the club took place yesterday? "
"What are you trying to say?"
"If you can't remember, then how do you know that it hasn't been longer ago?"
"I don't know, it feels like it was yesterday, OK? How about for you?" Shawn now wanted to know. "What exactly do you remember?"
"Nothing **in particular**," Justus replied hesitantly. "A completely normal school day. I came home, ate something, hung around the junkyard ... "
"Junkyard?"
"My uncle owns a second hand center. The Junkyard. Since I live with my uncle and my aunt, I spend most days there. In any case, I worked for my uncle, together with my colleague Peter. And from then on ... it all begins to **blur**. My memories are lost somewhere in the nothingness. I cannot even say what I did in the evening. "
He looked down at himself. He was still wearing the same old jeans, the T-shirt that was not completely clean anymore and sneakers whose **soles** were almost worn through and in one spot even broken. The shoes especially irritated him without

---

amnesia – Gedächtnisverlust;
in particular – im Besonderen, besonders;
to blur – verschwimmen;
soles – Sohlen

him being able to say why. "I haven't changed clothes since then at any rate. Strange. Really extremely strange."
"Strange," Shawn mimicked him, rolled his eyes and continued pacing through the room.
"Listen, Shawn: I know you're **confused** and **uncertain**. It's not any different for me. But nevertheless we should make an effort to work together. Maybe we can reconstruct what happened. Whom did you meet in that club, for example? Maybe that will help us."
"Look, man: your **drivel** is annoying. I just want to get out of here, OK? You can conduct your interview later."
Shawn stomped to the door and kicked furiously against it, before he slid with his back down it in frustration and pulled at his disheveled hair.
"Go ahead," said Justus **offended**. "You can try to kick in the door. I'm curious to see how far you get."
Shawn growled something unintelligible without looking up.
Justus sighed. Right now it probably made little sense to plan on Shawn's cooperation. Therefore he had to develop a strategy alone. The gray **steel door** was solid and **sealed**, the lock complicated. What other options were there?
Justus let his gaze wander. Just below the ceiling ran a **rusty water pipe**, about the width of an arm, that came out of the

---

confused – verwirrt;
uncertain – unsicher;
drivel – Gefasel, Geschwätz;
offended – beleidigt;
steel door – Stahltür;
sealed – verschlossen;
rusty water pipe – rostiges Wasserrohr

wall and that disappeared into the wall again at the other end of the room. Perhaps he could use one of the screws that connected the individual pieces of pipe as a tool for the door … no, that would not work.
The fluorescent tubes were **stained** and dusty. One of the stains, in the vague shape of an ax, reminded Justus of something. It was like a dream that came to the forefront of his memory for a split second. An island. A brown island that looked like an ax in a white sea …
But before Justus could **fully grasp the thought**, he was **distracted** by a sound. In the distance a **dull**, **reverberating stomping** could be heard. "Do you hear that too?"
"What?"
"Shhh!"
Justus crept to the door and put his car against the cold steel. There it was again: A **muted hammering**, like road construction that was five blocks away. Except that a strange, subterranean echo was mixed in with it. The sound came from a building. From this building. Then he had it: "Someone is **pounding** on a door!"

Jolene rattled on and on. She told Peter in great detail about yesterday evening, which she had spent watching TV with her little sister. What show they had watched. What flavor

---

stained – fleckig;
to fully grasp a thought – einen Gedanken richtig greifen;
to be distracted – abgelenkt sein;
dull, reverberating stomping – dumpfes, hallendes Stampfen;
muted hammering – gedämpftes Hämmern;
to pound – klopfen, hämmern

the chips had. When she had gone to her room. What book she had read. And for how long. That she had not gotten undressed and presumably had at some point simply fallen asleep.

Peter only half-listened. His head was clearing slowly, though. He still didn't know how he had gotten here. But at least the **dazed feeling** and **nausea** had almost disappeared. But the cold remained, creeping into his bones little by little.

"I dreamed some nonsense. I don't remember anymore … about my mother. I sat in a bus and … It really doesn't matter. Anyway, I woke up. And was here. Just like that. This … This is crazy, right? Maybe I'm schizophrenic or whatever that's called? Is this a padded cell? Or something else? Peter!"

"I don't know! I'm just as **clueless** as you! "

"But there must be an explanation!"

"There is one."

"What?"

"No idea. It's much more important that we get out of here first. I don't like this room."

"Tell me about it."

"Did you already attempt something while I was sleeping?" asked Peter.

"What do you mean?"

"Calling for help, for example."

Jolene shook her head.

Immediately Peter stood up, went to the steel door and pounded three or four times against it with his **fist**. The

---

dazed feeling – benommenes Gefühl; **nausea** – Übelkeit;
clueless – ratlos; **fist** – Faust;

tinny beating was uncomfortably loud in this bare room. Peter hoped that it was just as loud outside the door. He listened. Nothing. After a few seconds he started pounding again, longer this time.
But again there was no **response** from the other side. He'd better keep it up. At some point someone on the other side would notice him.
Jolene joined him and together they pounded, as loudly as they could, until their fists were red and numb. **Exhausted**, they took a break. At least the cold had disappeared from Peter's body for a moment.
"Do you think someone heard us?"
"If someone is nearby, definitely. The question is: Can that someone also help us?"
"Does that someone want to help us?" added Jolene. "If we really were kidnapped …" She shuddered.
A **tapping**. Far away.
"I heard something," whispered Peter.
The tapping was repeated.
"Someone's answering us," said Jolene so excited that her voice rose. She immediately rushed back to the door and shouted: "Help! Heeeelllppp!" She began to pound again, but this time with a **fervor** that frightened Peter.
"Help!!!"

---

tinny beating – blechernes Trommeln;
response – Antwort;
exhausted – erschöpft;
tapping – Pochen, Klopfen;
fervor – Inbrunst

"Jolene," said Peter, laying his hand on her shoulder. "Jolene, calm down!"
"I want to get out of here," she screamed and continued pounding.
"Jolene," Peter grabbed her arms and held her.
"What are you doing? Are you crazy? Let me go!"
"Jolene! If you keep making such a **racket**, we'll never find out what's going on out there!"
She **seethed with rage**. "What's going on? There's someone who can help us!"
"There is someone who has heard us, yes," agreed Peter. "So, you don't need to keep on pounding. But we likewise have to listen to him or her, do you understand? So pull yourself together and be quiet!"
Jolene glared at him angrily, but stopped protesting. Together, they held their breath. Yes, someone was knocking, without a doubt. But it was far away. And it wasn't getting closer. And it sounded just as desperate as their own attempt to attract attention.
After a while Peter said: "I don't know if I should be calm or **horrified** now. But it seems as if we're not the only prisoners here."

---

racket – Spektakel;
she seethed with rage – sie schäumte vor Wut;
horrified – entsetzt

Pipe Mail

"Wow, that really helped a lot," Shawn mocked after Justus had pounded on the door. "I'm impressed."
Justus decided not to let Shawn provoke him. The situation was too serious for them to want to go at each other. He only wanted one thing: to get out of here. And apparently there was someone out there somewhere who also wanted that. A vague sense of hope spread through his stomach. They were not alone. That was good. Because with some luck that meant that Bob and Peter were nearby. This idea occurred to Justus shortly after waking up. It didn't matter how Justus got into this **jam** – it **darn-well sure** smelled of a **case** that he had stumbled upon with his friends. It's true he could not remember, but … if Bob and Peter were nearby, then everything would be all right. Most definitely.
"We have to somehow communicate with the person who's knocking out there," said Justus finally.
"Sure, then go ahead and scream your heart out. It probably won't amount to much. Much too far away."
"I was thinking more of **tapping signals**," replied Justus.
Shawn laughed **scornfully**. "Do you want to tell me now that you know Morse code?"
"Precisely."
"Ha! Likely story. Are you in the army?"
Justus didn't acknowledge his comments. "The problem will

---

pipe mail – Rohrpost; **jam** – (hier) Lage, Situation;
darn-well sure – verdammt sicher; **case** – Fall;
tapping signals – Klopfzeichen; **scornfully** – verächtlich

be that the echoes of the tapping are so **muffled** that you can hardly **distinguish** one signal from another. It will be quite difficult to transmit a message."

"Should I tell you what will be difficult? Besides you, no one knows Morse code! It's not going to help you at all."

Justus shook his head. "I'll admit, I have no **evidence** for my **hunch**, but nevertheless I believe that my friends are nearby. And they could decipher my message."

Justus instantly regretted his words. For Shawn's **mockery** turned back into **cold fury** from one second to the next. "So, you do know something!" he hissed.

Justus involuntarily took two steps back. "Pardon? No, I – "

"Of course you know something! Why would you think that your friends are here otherwise? Tell me what's going on here finally! How did we get here? Who are you?"

"This is a misunderstanding! I really don't know where we are and how we got here. My hunch that my friends could be here is based only on the fact that we often find ourselves in threatening situations. We are detectives."

"Don't give me any crap!"

"That's the truth. I have a business card in my pants' pocket. Just a second ..." Justus rummaged in his pocket. But he found neither his card nor anything else. All of his pockets were completely empty. "My wallet! My **ID**! Someone must have removed everything."

Shawn looked reluctantly into his own pockets. "Me, too. But, you don't think that I believe your story for that reason."

---

muffled – dumpf; **to distinguish** – unterscheiden;
evidence – Beweis; **hunch** – Vermutung; **mockery** – Spott;
cold fury – kalte Wut; **ID** – Ausweis

"Now listen to me," said Justus angrily and took a step forward again with determination. "My friends and I have a detective agency. We have already been able to solve a number of mysterious cases. You can believe me or not, frankly it doesn't matter to me. But the fact of the matter is that I have a certain amount of experience in handling **disconcerting situations**. Therefore, it would be nice if you'd help me. Together, we'll get out of here faster. But if you want to **refuse**, please do. Somehow it'll work out without you, too."
Shawn silently looked at him. But slowly he seemed to understand that his **mistrust** also wasn't serving him well. "What are you planning?"
"I want to communicate with my friends, if they are out there. Nothing will come of the tapping signals, the acoustics are simply too bad. But I just thought about using that water pipe up there. Metal carries the signal farther more clearly and better than air. With some luck the pipe leads in the right direction. But I can't get to it alone. You have to help me."
Shawn frowned, looked first at Justus, then at the water pipe and finally back at Justus. "How's that going to work?"
"Let me get on your shoulders and I – "
"On my shoulders? You?" Shawn laughed for the first time and showed sparkling white teeth. "You definitely weigh …"
"Too much for you?" Justus's tone dripped with derision. "I actually thought you were an athletic, strong type. But I must have clearly been mistaken. There's really nothing more than hot air under your t-shirt, huh?"

---

disconcerting situation – befremdliche Situation;
to refuse – ablehnen; **mistrust** – Misstrauen

The amusement disappeared from Shawn's face as quickly as it had come. "All right, then. Get on. But hurry up!"
Shawn **squatted down** and Justus climbed on his shoulders. **Groaning**, Shawn struggled to stand up. His legs shook and he turned red until he finally stood up straight and could relax a little. "Now get started already!"
Justus knocked on the pipe. Two short, two long, two short. Pause. Two short, two long, two short. While doing so, he imagined the sound being carried through the pipe farther and farther, **branching out in all directions**, continuing through different rooms and buildings, until finally his distress signal was heard everywhere. A quite unrealistic idea, but it gave him **courage**. Two short, two long, two short.
"You keep tapping the same thing!" complained Shawn. "What is that, SOS? Doesn't it go differently somehow?"
"SOS would be three short, three long, three short," replied Justus and continued knocking incessantly. "But SOS is so well-known that even someone who hasn't mastered Morse code would recognize it. I don't want to attract attention from the wrong people."
"So, what is it then?"
"A question mark."
"What? The question mark? Can you please tell me **how the heck** a question mark is supposed to help us?"
"Just wait," replied Justus and kept tapping.

---

to squat down – in die Hocke gehen;
to groan – stöhnen, ächzen;
to branch out in all directions – in alle Richtungen verzweigen;
courage – Mut; **how the heck** – wie zur Hölle

"Wait? Listen up! You are not exactly a **flyweight** Justus!" Shawn suddenly started to **totter**. Justus tried to hold on to the pipe, but Shawn took two steps sideways, and Justus had to let go. This knocked both of them completely off balance, and suddenly Justus found himself in a free fall. He landed hard against the cold tiles. "Man! What was that?"
"I don't feel like it anymore," Shawn returned. "Question mark, such stupidity! I don't believe one single word! You're keeping something from me. I'm not stupid, though! What is this supposed to be, some kind of **mental game**? You know what, though? Keep playing alone! I'm not playing along anymore!" Shawn returned to the corner where Justus had first seen him an hour before, sat down and glared at him grimly.
Justus sighed. How could he **convince** Shawn now? Whatever Justus did or said seemed only to **strengthen** his **distrust**. Maybe he should really continue alone and act as if Shawn didn't exist at all. Then at least he wouldn't be in danger of falling again.
But before Justus had even decided, his attention was **diverted**. A hollow, metallic **rattling** interrupted the silence. Simultaneously, Justus and Shawn turned their gazes to the water pipe. The signal was not very loud, but for that, all the more clear.
Two short, two long, two short.
Justus smiled. "I think we have pipe mail."

---

flyweight – Fliegengewicht ; **to totter** – wanken;
mental game – Psychospiel(chen);
to convince – überzeugen;
to strengthen – stärken; **distrust** – Unglaube;
to divert – ablenken; **rattling** – Knacken, Klopfen

Contact

One short, four long. Pause. Short, long, short, long, short, long. Pause. Two short, two long, two short.

Peter let go of the water pipe and landed with a bounce on the floor. He was grinning from ear to ear.

"Now what was that?" Jolene asked.

"One, period, question mark," Peter translated the signal that he had just **transmitted**.

"One, period, question mark? What's that supposed to mean?"

Peter squatted down and drew the symbols in the **grime** that covered the floor: 1.?

"First of all?" wondered Jolene out loud.

"First?" corrected Peter. "I just asked whether I'm speaking with Justus. He is the First Detective, you know. 'First, is that you?' That's about how I meant my signal. I am sure he'll understand it. If it's him."

"Detective?" asked Jolene blankly.

Before Peter could reply, the answer was already coming: one short, three long. Pause. One short, one long. Yes.

Peter jumped up in the air. "It's Justus! It's really Justus! Jolene, we're **rescued**!"

"I … I don't understand. Who is Justus?"

"Justus is the smartest person under the sun. And he is somewhere nearby. He will get us out of here. For sure."

---

to transmit – übermitteln;
grime – Schmutz, Schmierfilm;
rescued – gerettet

Immediately Peter jumped up to the water pipe, held tight with one hand and with the other hand transmitted a new message. Then he dropped back down again and waited anxiously for the response. So back and forth it went. Due to the **arduousness of the transmission**, the **exchange** took place in telegram form.
Clack. Clack. Clack. Stop. Clack. Clack. Clack. Stop. Clack. Clackclackclack. Stop. Clackclack. Stop. Clackclackclack. Stop. Clack. Stop. Clack. Clackclack. Stop. Clackclack. Clack.
Like a **woodpecker** on a tree trunk, Peter diligently tapped one message after the next and translated the slow-moving conversation bit by bit for a tense Jolene.
And so steadily, like a woodpecker hollows out the wood, the First Detective's responses hollowed out Peter's hope, until at last they lay on the ground like **finely carved shavings**.
– peter here. where are you? –
– trapped. no windows. door shut. –
– me too. white room. two of us. –
– likewise. bob? –
– no. with you? –
– no. where is he? –
– n. i.– (that meant "no idea".)
– what happened? –
– n. i.–
– memory gone? –
– yes. –
– likewise. –

---

arduousness of the transmission – Mühseligkeit der Übermittlung;
exchange – Austausch; **woodpecker** – Specht;
finely carved shavings – fein zerbröselte Späne

– escape options? –
– no. your picklock set? –
– gone. what now? –
– n. i.–
Again, Shawn began to **stagger**.
"Don't drop me again!" warned Justus.
"Then kindly hurry up!" Shawn groaned. "I can't hold you much longer!"
"Just a second", retorted Justus and tapped one last message.
– tool in the vi –
Shawn legs **buckled**. Justus was clinging to the tube and suddenly hanging in the air, his face pressed against the greasy white tiled wall.
"Sorry," mumbled Shawn.
"Your apology doesn't help me any," Justus groaned and considered what was more inelegant: to drop like a wet bag or to remain hanging like a piece of meat on a hook until Shawn **bailed him out**.
The decision was **moot**, because all of a sudden it creaked and cracked, and with dust and **plaster** raining down an **anchor** tore from the wall. The pipe broke in half and crashed down along with the First Detective. For the second time within a few minutes, he landed extremely roughly. Putrid, brown water splashed out of the hole in the wall for a few seconds before it **petered out**.

---

to stagger – taumeln; **to buckle** – einknicken;
to bail s.o. out – jmd. aus der Patsche helfen;
moot – hinfällig, strittig; **plaster** – Putz, Gips;
anchor – Verankerung; **to peter out** – versiegen

With difficulty, Justus picked himself up. Shawn just looked silently at him. He didn't even **grin derisively**. He left Justus all alone in his disgrace, which made the First Detective all the more furious. "I'm all right, thanks for your concern." He looked up. A piece of pipe was still sticking out of the wall. It shouldn't be a problem to continue communicating with Peter. On the contrary: Justus could now use the broken piece for tapping and therefore was no longer dependent on Shawn's assistance. But as he turned to complete his message, he stopped short.
Something was hanging on the ceiling. A black box. Neither Justus nor Shawn had previously noticed it, since the pipe's **shadow** had hidden it. But now that the pipe had broken off, it was hard to miss. Justus went closer to it and **squinted**. The thing was about half as big as a shoebox, dull black and made of metal.
Then he realized what it was.

The fear he had felt after his awakening was abruptly there again. Cold, almost palpable fear spread slowly from the pit of his stomach through his whole body like freezing water. Suddenly he was conscious of the cold in the room again, he got **goose bumps**. With a trembling hand he pointed to the object on the ceiling.
Shawn discovered it now, too. And Justus watched on his face as the same change occurred. "It … it can't be."
"Unfortunately, there's hardly a doubt," replied the First Detective with a hoarse voice. "Either everything here, this room,

---

to grin derisively – höhnisch grinsen; **shadow** – Schatten;
to squint – die Augen zusammenkneifen; **goose bumps** – Gänsehaut

the whole situation is a big joke, which I unfortunately don't understand. Or the situation is much more dangerous and unpredictable than we could have ever suspected until now."

Peter jumped up, held onto the water pipe with one hand and tapped a message with the other.
– still there? –
Then he dropped and looked up concerned. Justus had stopped mid-sentence. Then, there was a disquietingly loud noise. Since then, there was a deathly silence.
Spellbound, they waited for a response. Finally, after a few minutes the tapping resumed. Peter breathed a **sigh of relief**.
"What is it?" asked Jolene impatiently. "What's he saying?"
Peter concentrated on the Morse code and finally translated: "'Sorry. Was distracted. Room searched?' Room searched? What does he mean by that?"
"Well, whether we have searched the room."
"But there's nothing here to search. It's empty." Once again Peter swung himself up and tapped out a short – yes. –
The answer came promptly: – above the pipe? –
Peter **frowned** and stood on his **tiptoes**.
"What's the matter?"
"Justus thinks we should take a look above the pipe." He took a few steps back and jumped into the air, in order to take a look into the dark area that lay between the pipe and ceiling. But there was nothing there. Peter walked backward until his back hit the cold, greasy tiles and stood on his tiptoes. Then he saw it. In the back, on the right, something was hanging

---

spellbound – gebannt; **sigh of relief** – Seufzer der Erleichterung;
to frown – die Stirn runzeln; **tiptoes** – Zehenspitzen

just below the ceiling. A box. Black and dull and outfitted with a tiny red light that was pulsating. On the front of the box was something round and shiny. A lens.
The shock was so great that Peter held his breath, horrified.
"What is it?" asked Jolene concerned and followed Peter's gaze. Then she saw it, too.
"A camera!" exclaimed Peter. "We … we are being filmed! I can't believe it!"
The security camera was positioned in such a way that about three quarters of the room was in the **frame**. When Peter had overcome his initial shock, he moved immediately out of the camera's range. "Jolene!" he whispered and waved the girl over to him. "Come here!"
Jolene was visibly annoyed, but then followed him.
"We were being observed the whole time," whispered Peter. "Possibly even **eavesdropped on**! The camera is equipped with a microphone for sure. I just don't get it! What does it mean?"
"What …? I … I don't know."
Peter feverishly thought it over. They were being **monitored**. By whom? Why? What was going on here? What should he do now? Talk with the person who was sitting on the other end and watching them? If someone even sat there at all. Perhaps everything was just being recorded.
Tapping on the pipe tore him from his thoughts. – everything okay? – Peter translated and hurried to tell Justus about his discovery.

---

frame – Bild;
to eavesdrop on s.o. – jmd. belauschen;
to monitor – überwachen

– Camera found! –
– Not just you. –
– ??? –
– !!!–
– what now? –
– turn it off! –
Turn it off. Of course. Peter would have figured that out himself, too. He had kept well clear of the camera as if it were a bomb. It was as if the enemy, whom Peter had suspected was out there somewhere, had suddenly entered. Identity and motive were as mysterious as before, but now it was certain: Someone was there. Someone who was watching them. Who had followed their every step up until now. An unknown presence that made a show of its **superiority** via the camera. The **perpetrator** knew who they were, what they did and what they said. Peter and Jolene, in contrast, knew nothing.
The Second Detective broke out of his **paralysis**. He ran toward the camera and jumped up. His fingers brushed the box. But that was not enough.
"Peter, what … what are you doing?"
"You have to ask? Jolene, we're being watched!"
"Yes, but …"
"But what?"
Jolene didn't answer. Peter frowned. What **objections** could she have? The Second Detective didn't want to be watched and eavesdropped on for a second longer! Shaking his head, he turned again toward the camera. It was hanging too high to be able to reach it with a pull-up on the pipe.

---

superiority – Überlegenheit; **perpetrator** – Täter;
paralysis – Lähmung, Starre; **objection** –Einwand

But not so high that it was out of reach. He wasn't one of the best players on the school's basketball team for nothing.
Peter walked to the farthest corner of the room. The camera lens now had him in full view. Peter looked at it enraged.
"Hasta la vista, baby," he snarled and began his **approach**. Two, three long steps, then the jump. Peter flew through the air, took a swing and hit the lens with his clenched fist.
The **surveillance camera** broke away from its attachment and then bobbed from a cable on the ceiling. Now Peter could reach it without a problem. He hit it again and the camera sailed clear across the room. Splintering apart, **it kicked the bucket**. The red flashing light went out.

---

approach – Annäherung, Anlauf;
surveillance camera – Überwachungskamera;
to kick the bucket – sterben

Under Observation

Justus weighed the camera in his hand, inspecting it. It looked like a surveillance camera like in banks or department stores, just somewhat less **bulky**. The First Detective had been successful in **detaching** it without damaging it in the process. He only had to tear out the cable that had led from the camera into the wall. The transmission was thereby interrupted. Whoever had been watching them the last hour – he now saw nothing more.

Shawn walked up and first looked at the camera, then Justus's face. His expression was hard to read.

"Now Big Brother's got a problem," Justus said.

"Hopefully his problem won't become ours."

"What do you mean by that?"

Again Shawn looked at Justus as if he were seeing him for the first time.

"What's up?" asked Justus.

Shawn shook his head without a word and turned away.

But Justus's ears **perked up**. Something was going on. Justus just didn't know what.

"Would you be kind enough to answer me?"

"What?" Shawn asked irritably. "What do you want to know?"

"I want to know what you think of all this. About the camera, I mean. About the fact that someone has been watching us over the last hour."

"That's something, yeah," was the dispassionate answer. "And?"

---

bulky – klobig, sperrig; **to detach** – abmontieren;
to perk up – hellhörig werden

“Well, now we know that we didn’t end up here **on accident**!”
“Not on accident! You don’t say! You **seldom** accidentally **wind up** in a warehouse and can’t remember anything!”
Justus frowned. “In a warehouse? Where did you get the idea that we’re in a warehouse?”
“Who knows! It was just a thought! It looks like a warehouse, doesn’t it? Don’t get on my nerves now! Instead, figure out how we’re getting out of here! I think you’re such a wonderful detective! What’s up with your friend on the other side? Banging on a water pipe isn’t helping us anymore!”
Justus nodded and turned toward the pipe again. Shawn was hiding something from him, he was sure about that. But it was better if he knew nothing of Justus’s **suspicion**.
The First Detective concentrated and tapped out the next message to Peter.

“What’s your friend saying?” Jolene wanted to know. But Peter **hesitated** with the translation. Had he understood that correctly?
– trust no one! –
Justus could actually only mean Jolene by that. Which meant that Peter really shouldn’t translate this message. “He …he’s asking if I was successful,” answered Peter hesitating and tapped a quick – OK – back. Then he looked at the remains of the camera that still lay **untouched** in the corner. He had an idea.

---

on accident – zufällig; **seldom** – selten;
to wind up – hineingeraten; **suspicion** – Verdacht;
to hesitate – zögern; **untouched** – unberührt

"This camera ...," he murmured and picked it up.
"What about it?"
"It's made of metal."
"Yeah. Sure."
"And it's already broken anyway."
"Right. So what?"
Peter dropped the camera. Then he lifted his right foot and let the heel of his sneaker whiz down on the **casing** with all his might. With an **ear-deafening crunch** the expensive piece of technology cracked. Peter stepped on it again. And then again. After the fourth time the casing finally lay in fragments before him, revealing its insides. Like the skeleton of a dead animal, cables and **circuit boards** stuck out of the wreckage. Jolene was stunned. "Are you completely **insane**? What are you doing? We could have still used that thing!"
"Yeah, sure. We'll make it so nice and cozy here inside and shoot a short home video."
"That's not what I mean! But can you now explain to me how doing that made sense?"
"Yeah," said Peter and bent down to the individual pieces of the camera. "I can." **Layer by layer** he **dissected** the camera's insides and rummaged through the cable salad, until he had finally found what he was looking for: a small **metal clip** that had held the circuit board in place in the casing. On the other side he found a second very similar metal piece. Triumphant-

---

casing – Gehäuse;
ear-deafening crunch – ohrenbetäubendes Knirschen;
circuit board – Platine; **insane** – verrückt;
layer by layer – Schicht für Schicht; **to dissect** – freilegen;
metal clip – Metallbügel

ly he held both of them up. “With some luck, this is our way out.”
Hope and doubt were mirrored in Jolene’s gaze. “Now what’s that supposed to mean?”
Peter walked to the steel door and **investigated** the lock more closely. He tentatively stuck the metal clip in the keyhole, felt around inside with it, pulled the clip out again and **bent** a small part into a **right angle** with his teeth.
“Wait a second! Will you get the lock open somehow?”
“Like I already said: with some luck.”
“That’s ... that’s great! But why do you know how to do that? First Morse code and now this too! Does this have to do with that detective stuff, too?”
“Well, a little,” answered Peter. In the meantime, he had told Jolene a bit about die drei ???. While he had bent both metal clips for his purposes and tried them out, he continued: “Our headquarters, the command center, is located at Justus’s uncle’s scrapyard. And there are always **loads of** old doors and **dismantled locks** lying around. At some point I started to occupy myself with them.”
“How?”
“To pick locks. It’s not that difficult at all if you already know how it works. Aha ... now I’ve got you!”
“Are you unlocking it?” asked Jolene full of hope.
“Not yet. But at least I know how the mechanism is built. It might still take a while.”
“Do you think you’ll do it?”

---

to investigate – untersuchen; **to bend** – (ver-)biegen;
right angle – rechter Winkel; **loads of** – eine Menge;
dismantled locks – ausgebaute Schlösser

"We'll see." Peter got to work.
"This Third Detective that you talked about," Jolene continued with **curiosity**. "Do you think he's also here?"
"Bob," said Peter. "I don't know. It doesn't seem that he's with Justus. I didn't see him at all in the last few days, so I don't know whether … I simply can't remember, do you understand? I hope he's well." Peter **became queasy** thinking about Bob. He had been so **relieved** to receive a sign of life from Justus! That he didn't yet have one from Bob could be a good sign. Or a **darned bad** one.
Click.
Peter froze. The lock mechanism in the **interior** of the lock had **relented**.
"What is it?" Jolene asked excitedly.
Peter involuntarily lowered his voice. "I think … the door is open!"

The sun was burning so hot this afternoon that Bob Andrews was happy when he could turn his bike onto the **property** of Titus Jonas's Second Hand Center and duck into the high wooden fence's cool shadows. His sunshine yellow VW Beetle that he had lent Justus and Peter because Peter's car was broken, was standing nearby. So, both of them were probably here.
He had just gotten off the seat when Mathilda Jonas, Justus's

---

curiosity – Neugier; **to become queasy** – mulmig werden;
to be relieved – erleichtert sein; **darned bad** – verdammt schlecht;
interior – das Innere; **to relent** – nachgeben;
property – Besitz, Eigentum

aunt, came running **in a tizzy**. "Bob! Bob Andrews! Thank God that you're finally here! Bob!"
Stunned, Bob turned toward Aunt Mathilda. "What's the matter, Mrs. Jonas?"
"Bob!" Aunt Mathilda reached him out of breath. "Do you know where Justus is?"
"Justus? No. I had hoped he would be here."
"And Peter?"
"I have absolutely no idea. Why? Has something happened?"
"If something's happened?" Aunt Mathilda's voice escalated to hysteria. She grabbed his shoulders. "You really don't know then what I'm talking about? Are you serious? Don't joke with me, Bob Andrews!"
Bob was slowly getting **scared** now. "It's not a joke. I was at my aunt's in Idaho for three days with my parents. We just got back half an hour ago. I immediately got on my bike and rode here to see if there was anything new."
"There's something new, for sure!" exclaimed Aunt Mathilda. "Justus has disappeared! And Peter too!"
"Disappeared? What's that supposed to mean?"
"That they're gone! This morning I wondered why Justus didn't want to get up at all. So I went into his room in order to wake him. But he wasn't there! He wasn't there the whole night!"
"Maybe he just got up early."
But Aunt Mathilda decisively shook her head. "His bed was made. Justus never makes his bed. I always make it. That means he hasn't lain in it since yesterday. Immediately I called

---

in a tizzy – in heller Aufregung; **stunned** – verwundert;
scared – verängstigt, ängstlich

the Shaws and your parents. At your house no one was home, but I reached Mrs. Shaw. And now guess! Peter has also disappeared! Please, Bob, if you know something, then you have to tell me!"

Before Bob could answer, Uncle Titus hurried over no less **agitated** than his wife. "And?" he exclaimed. "What's up? Do you know where they are, Bob?"

"No, I ... I'm sorry, Mr. Jonas, I'm **completely stumped**. I can't explain what happened."

"But that does have something to do with your detective games!" ranted Aunt Mathilda. "**Don't kid with me**!"

"We weren't working on any case at all when I went to Idaho. When I saw Justus and Peter the last time on Wednesday we just played computer games. Everything was perfectly OK."

"But that can't be!" said Uncle Titus and nervously twirled his massive black walrus mustache. "Where could they possibly be?"

"What was last night?" asked Bob. "Did Justus say anything?"

"Everything was like it always is!" Aunt Mathilda **assured** him. "Titus and I watched a murder mystery and Justus said good night. That was around ten. Then he went to his room."

"Did you check on him again after that?"

"Please!" said Aunt Mathilda **indignantly**. "Do you think that I check every night to see if he's covered up correctly? He's not a baby anymore! Besides that, he usually goes to bed after us. Just not last night."

---

agitated – aufgeregt; **I am completely stumped** – Ich bin völlig ratlos; **don't kid with me** – mach mir nichts vor;
to assure – versichern, mitteilen; **indignantly** – entrüstet

"You know what," said Bob and forced himself to smile. "Everything will probably get cleared up quite simply. I'm sure that Justus got up this morning very early in order to take care of something completely harmless. And to make you happy he made his bed himself."

"He didn't eat breakfast!" **retorted** Aunt Mathilda vigorously. "I could tell that by the orange juice bottle. It's just as full as it was yesterday. And Justus without breakfast? That's completely impossible. So he wasn't at home during the night. That is ... a logical conclusion, right? I've learned a little bit from your detective stuff."

"Bob, you must know something! Where is our boy? We already wanted to check in your **trailer**, but we don't have a key."

"Calm down!" Bob said as insistently as possible. "Nothing has happened to Justus and Peter, of that I'm quite sure. I'll go into headquarters now and see if I find a message or something like that. Don't worry!" He smiled encouragingly.

The smile only disappeared from Bob's face when he had turned around and was heading toward headquarters. He had no idea what was going on here. He was relatively certain that Aunt Mathilda was right about her suspicions. Justus hadn't spent last night in his bed. And there was only one logical explanation for that: Justus and Peter had been on a nightly **reconnaissance mission**. Unfortunately, Bob had absolutely no idea why and wherefore. That meant that something must have happened while he had been in Idaho. Justus and Peter had slid into a new case, had spent last night investigating – and something had gone wrong. Totally, tremendously wrong.

---

to retort – widersprechen; **trailer** – Wohnwagen;
reconnaissance mission – nächtliche Erkundungstour

Evil Games

The desk was overflowing with paper. There were mountains of newspapers stacked on the floor. Dirty dishes were piled high in the tiny sink. Empty pizza boxes were lying on chairs and armchairs' armrests. Headquarters looked like it always did. At first glance there was nothing to indicate that something **out of the ordinary** had **occurred** in the three days of Bob's absence. But why would it?

The answering machine was blinking and displayed seven incoming calls. There! Bob listened to the messages. But the results were disappointing: seven times no one had left a message, but rather had hung up again immediately.

"And?" a voice behind him said. Bob flinched. Aunt Mathilda and Uncle Titus stood in the doorway and watched him full of hope. He hadn't even noticed that they had followed him.

"Well, I don't see anything out of the ordinary at first glance. I'll see if I can find a message somewhere." Bob turned around again. The Jonas couple made no move to disappear. "This might take a while," Bob added, but still there was no reaction from either of them. Bob half-heartedly lifted up a couple of piles of paper and moved pieces of paper on the desk, but the presence of Aunt Mathilda and Uncle Titus made him so nervous that he couldn't concentrate.

"We'll help you," said Aunt Mathilda and took a step into headquarters.

---

evil – teuflisch;
out of the ordinary – etwas Außergewöhnliches;
to occur – vorfallen, geschehen

"No!" Bob exclaimed louder than he had intended. "I mean, it would be better if you didn't. "You see, headquarters is ..." ... Our sanctuary where adults don't belong, went through his head. But of course he couldn't say that. "It's like a **delicate habitat**. Everything has its place and may not be cleared away. It's better if I do it myself. Thank you."

Disappointed Aunt Mathilda **retreated**. "But you'll tell us immediately when you've found something!" she urged him.

Bob nodded, smiling. "Yes, of course."

Finally, the Jonas couple trudged away. Relieved, Bob closed the door and breathed deeply. Then he let his eyes roam over the chaos. The desk. If there were notes that Justus or Peter had made, then he would most likely find them there. He began to **comb through** the pieces of paper.

After the desk came the papers lying on the floor and the books were next. Then the **lab** located in the back section of the trailer. And finally the files on the computer. Bob checked everything that had been used in the last three days, including Internet access. None of it helped him in any way. Except for a scribbled note in Justus's handwriting on a piece of paper. An address and a telephone number that were both **unfamiliar** to him.

Bob thoughtfully looked at the paper. Did it have anything at all to do with Justus's and Peter's **disappearance**? There was

---

delicate habitat – empfindliche Umgebung;
to retreat – sich zurückziehen;
to comb through – durchkämmen;
lab – Labor; **unfamiliar** – unbekannt;
disappearance – Verschwinden

only one way to figure that out. Bob reached for the telephone and dialed the unknown number. It rang three times, then a masculine voice answered.

"Hello, you've reached the office of William Boyd. I'm currently not at my desk. You can reach me mornings between ten and twelve o'clock. If the matter is urgent, please leave a message after the tone." Beep.

"Uh … hi, this is Bob Andrews. We don't know each other, but …" Bob froze. He couldn't just tell this stranger that he was searching for Justus Jonas and Peter Shaw! What if this William Boyd was responsible for their disappearance? Bob had no idea what kind of business his friends were wrapped up in. "… but it would be nice if you called me back." Bob left the number for headquarters and hung up. He hesitated. That had been a mistake, he knew it. But before he could more thoroughly contemplate it, the phone rang. Bob's heart jumped. William Boyd? Maybe he had just come back to the office and was immediately returning the call. But what should he tell him? But maybe it was Justus, too! Yeah, exactly! The First Detective had sensed that Bob was at headquarters and was calling him now to explain everything.

Bob grabbed the phone. "Hello?"

"Bob! Hi! You're back!"

It wasn't Justus. It also wasn't William Boyd. It was Jelena, die drei ???'s friend. More specifically, Bob's friend.

"Jelena," groaned the Third Detective. "It's you. Tell me, did you call here seven times?"

"That's some kind of greeting," griped Jelena. "No, I didn't. Is there anything else?"

"I'm sorry. Don't take it personally. I had hoped you were Justus."

"Of course. A telephone call from your boss whom you see

on average sixteen hours a day is more important than anything else."

"You don't understand, Jelena. Justus is gone. And Peter, too. Since last night already. No one knows where they are. Including me. In fact, I just got back today from Idaho."

"Gone?" asked Jelena in surprise. "Now, that's something. I talked with Justus on the phone yesterday, though."

"You did what?"

"Yeah. Of course, I actually wanted to talk to you, not Justus."

"When exactly was that, Jelena? And what did Justus say?"

Jelena thought a moment. "That must have been about four o'clock. Justus just told me that you were visiting relatives and wanted to hang up already again in order not to have to talk with me one second longer than necessary. But to annoy him, I involved him in a conversation. I asked him if you guys were working on a new case, etc."

"And what did he say?"

"As a matter of fact, we are," Jelena **mimicked** the First Detective's **cadence**. "And for that reason, now it's unfortunately not possible for me to continue our conversation, Jelena. We have **to tail** a suspicious individual, in fact."

"A suspicious individual? Who?"

"He didn't reveal that to me, of course."

"Do you know what it was about?"

"You know that Justus doesn't like to divulge details. And definitely not to me. You really are worried, aren't you?"

"Of course I'm worried! His aunt and his uncle just **ambushed**

---

on average – im Durchschnitt ; **to mimick** – nachahmen;
cadence – Tonfall; **to tail** – beschatten;
to ambush – belagern

me. They're totally **distraught**. I have to do something. But I don't know what."
"Did you search headquarters already?"
"I just finished."
"And?"
Bob sighed. "I found a piece of paper. With a telephone number and an address. I already called the number, the answering machine answered for a certain William Boyd, whom I've never heard of."
"And what's the address?"
"32 Richmond Road."
"And? Does that mean anything to you?"
"No. Richmond Road is in West Hollywood. Swanky area. But I have no idea who might live there."
"Well, what are you waiting for then? Find out!"

32 Richmond Road was an apartment building built in Spanish style with a pale yellow exterior and a reddish brown shingle roof. It was on a street lined with royal palms **directly adjacent** to a park. The balconies facing the street were **deserted**. Only one woman on the second floor was sitting in a leopard-print bathing suit wearing sunglasses and holding her apparently freshly painted fingernails out to dry in the sun.
Bob, who had stopped on the street, cast a skeptical glance out the side window of his old VW Beetle. He had hoped that something different would **be concealed behind** the address on Justus's piece of paper – a business, for example. A restau-

---

distraught – verzweifelt;
directly adjacent – direkt neben; **deserted** – verlassen;
to be concealed behind – sich hinter etw. verbergen

rant, a company, an office, whatever. But this was a completely ordinary apartment building. How was Bob supposed to find out what Justus and Peter had wanted here? If they had even been here at all. He had already taken a lap around the whole building and had read the names on the **doorbell panels** without coming up with anything. Now he was sitting in his car again and thinking how he should **proceed**. Bob was completely lost in his thoughts when suddenly a hand pounded against the driver's side window!
"Jelena!"
"Hi. Am I too late?"
"What are you doing here?"
"What do you think? I'm supporting you in your detective duties. But must we discuss this through the window or may I come in?"
Bob nodded **dumbfounded** and opened the passenger door. Jelena went around the car and began to get into the car. Since an accident in her childhood, the girl had been a **paraplegic** and sat in a **wheelchair**, but transferring to the car was not a problem for Jelena.
"How did you get here?"
"How do you think? I drove!"
Bob looked at the wheelchair that was standing outside on the sidewalk.
"Not with that. With a taxi, of course. I did have the address. Did you find out anything yet? Any **tracc** of William Boyd?"

---

doorbell panels – Klingelschilder; **to proceed** – weitermachen; **dumbfounded** – verdattert; **paraplegic** – Querschnittsgelähmte; **wheelchair** – Rollstuhl; **trace** – Spur

Bob shook his head. "It's nice of you that you want to help me. But I'm afraid there isn't anything that I need help with. This is Richmond Road, great, but there's nothing here to help us."
"And if we ask the **residents** of the apartment building about Justus and Peter?"
"Just like that? There are at least a **dozen** apartments inside. Are we supposed to ring the doorbell at all of them? That's not a good idea, Jelena. We might only make everything worse by doing that."
"What do you think happened? Were they both kidnapped?"
"If I only knew! I don't have the slightest idea. But Aunt Mathilda and Peter's parents are going to **involve** the police by tonight at the latest, if I haven't found out anything by then. I – "
Bonk!
Bob flinched. The dull, metallic sound had been very close. He looked around. A boy was riding by on a skateboard just then. Other than that the street was deserted. "Did you hear that, too?"
"I'm not deaf," answered Jelena. "Sounded like someone –"
Bonk!
"Had pounded on my car's roof!" Bob completed the sentence and angrily looked upward through the **windshield**. He couldn't see anything. "But how can that –"
Bonk! A rotten, squashed orange slid from the roof down the window, leaving behind a line of smeared wetness.

---

residents – Bewohner;
a dozen – ein Dutzend; **to involve** – einbeziehen, einschalten;
windshield – Windschutzscheibe

Crazy Woman

In no time flat Bob had gotten out of his car. On his roof were two more oranges whose shiny gray **peels** had busted open. Bob looked around furiously, but still he couldn't find anyone.

Splat!

The next orange landed on the hot asphalt and narrowly missed the VW and its driver. But this time Bob could figure out where the shot had come from. He looked up. The woman in the leopard dress who had been sunning herself on her balcony held a bowl of oranges in her hand and was already **taking aim** with the next one.

"Hey! Stop that!"

"Finally you'll disappear!" she nagged with a strangely sing-song voice. "Go, get out of here, you horrible Paparazzi! There's nothing to see here! And take the wheel chair with you, OK!"

Bob was so **flabbergasted** by the woman's **brazenness** that he was speechless for a second.

Jelena was therefore faster. She rolled down the window and shouted, "Are you still all there, young woman? Or did the sun fry your brain?"

"I'm tired of you constantly hanging around my house!"

"Your house?" answered Bob.

---

in no time flat – in null Komma nichts;
peels – Schalen; **to take aim** – zielen;
flabbergasted – verblüfft;
brazenness – Unverschämtheit

"Yes, my house, who else's? **I'm not broke** despite what's in the newspapers! That you reporters can't leave a star like me in peace! And now go already or I'll call the police!"
"First of all, we're on a public street and we can stay here as long as we want. And second of all … I don't even know who you are."
"Ha!" the woman blurted hysterically. It almost sounded like a laugh. "And I'm supposed to believe that? I know exactly what you have planned! You'll hang around here again for hours to watch me and to shoot sneaky pictures! In order to sell them to the newspapers!"
"I'm sorry, but you must have us confused. We don't want to take any pictures. We don't even have a camera with us."
"Oh, no?" said the woman and leaned so far over the balcony railing that she would've made an excellent photo subject. It almost looked like she was waiting for Bob to pull out a camera and shoot. "And yesterday you didn't have a camera with you either, right?"
"Yesterday?"
"Yes, yesterday. Or do you think that I don't recognize your car?"
At that moment it dawned on Bob. "The car!" he whispered to Jelena.
"What about the car?" she whispered back.
"I **lent** the VW to Justus and Peter for the time that I was away, because Peter's MG is in the repair shop. The crazy woman up there recognized the car! That means …" Bob didn't complete his thought, but rather more loudly addressed

---

to be broke – pleite sein; **to lend** – ausleihen

the woman on the balcony, who had just struck a new pose. "When would we have been standing here in your opinion?"
"Well, yesterday afternoon, you **smart alec**! For hours! And then you followed poor Jonathan too! But the photo editors must not have been happy with the pictures, huh? I didn't find them in any newspaper this morning in any case. And now you're here to take new ones. But not of me!" She tossed her blond curls over her shoulder and pushed her sunglasses into her hair.
"Jonathan?" Bob asked as casually as possible.
"Yes, Jonathan!" the woman retorted angrily. "Jonathan Thorndike, now don't act so innocent! So now, are you leaving **voluntarily** or should I call the police?"
"We're leaving," answered Bob. "But you can be happy that I'm not calling the police because of you. Luckily the oranges didn't leave any **dents** in my roof."
"You ... you're really going to leave?" The crazy woman didn't even attempt to hide her **bewilderment**. Then she suddenly became furious. "You **darned brats**! Take a picture of me! Get me in the paper! Come on!" She reached for another piece of fruit that she held out threateningly.
Bob rushed to get into the car. "The old woman's lost her marbles!" He started the engine.
"Hey, my wheelchair!" called Jelena and opened the door.
"We'll meet up behind the building, OK?"
Jelena nodded and climbed out of the car. As soon as she was securely sitting in the wheelchair, Bob **accelerated**. He drove

---

smart alec – Schlauberger; **voluntarily** – freiwillig;
dents – Dellen; **bewilderment** – Fassungslosigkeit;
darned brats – verdammte Gören; **to accelerate** – beschleunigen

to the next street corner and turned right. He met Jelena again on the other side of the apartment building.
"My goodness, Hollywood! Really only crazy stars, ex-stars and those who think of themselves as such live here. That woman seemed to belong to the third category."
"Nevertheless, I don't believe that she was lying. She saw my car yesterday in front of the apartments. Justus and Peter must have been here! And we also know what they were looking for here: to observe Jonathan Thorndike, otherwise they wouldn't have driven after him. I saw his name before on the doorbell panel, Jelena: this Thorndike lives here!"
"And who is he? Yet another pseudostar?"
"I have no idea. But we'll find out!"
But **it was not as easy a task** as Bob had imagined it would be. There was only one entrance to the building. And that entrance was **barred** for one thing and for another it was **guarded** by the crazy woman. "There's only one possibility," said the Third Detective as they stood at the back of the building on the wall that surrounded the property. "I have to climb over."
Bob avoided looking at the wheelchair.
"Climb over?" echoed Jelena. "Well, great! And what about me?"
"You'll stay here. After all –"
"We can simply ring Thorndike's doorbell and enter the building the normal way!" Jelena interrupted him gruffly. "That stupid woman on the balcony **can kiss my butt**!"

---

it was not as easy a task – es war kein leichtes Unterfangen;
barred – versperrt; **guarded** – bewacht;
she can kiss my butt – sie kann mich mal

"That's too dangerous, Jelena. We don't even know who this Thorndike is and what he had to do with Justus's and Peter's disappearance. And as long as we don't –"
"**You're full of it**! The truth is that the poor, **disabled** Jelena is in the way again with her wheelchair, when the great detective does his investigative work. Awesome, Bob! But, you know what? I'm not your **slave**. I can do what I want. And I want to be there when –"
"Shhh!" said Bob, laid his finger beseechingly on his lips, grabbed Jelena's wheelchair and pushed her a couple of meters away from the wall.
"What, are you crazy?!" Jelena said indignantly, but Bob didn't respond.
"So, first of all," he whispered insistently, "not so loud! Second of all: you know that you're talking nonsense, Jelena. You're not in the way. But as long as we can't tell what's going on in this situation, it's better if only one of us puts ourselves in danger. And that should be the person who can get away quicker in the case of an emergency. **For safety's sake**, you stay here and get help if something goes wrong."
"You're already talking like Justus," snarled Jelena and crossed her arms angrily.
"And you should get out of the **habit** of always playing your wheelchair-sympathy-card in order to get your way." Bob bit his lip. Maybe it would have been better if he had kept that to himself, even though he meant exactly that. Jelena could get

---

you're full of it – du spinnst; **disabled** – behindert;
slave – Sklave; **for safety's sake** – zur Sicherheit;
habit – Gewohnheit

really angry, even violently so. Tense and anxious he waited for her reaction.
She looked at him angrily for a moment. But then her mouth gave way to a small grin. "**That hit home**," she said. "If Justus had said that, I would be unleashing a whole load of biting, poisonous and radioactive come-backs at him now. But because it's you ... I'll let this **impudence** go this time. Now, get out of here already! If I hear your cries of death, I'll rush to help you with my battle horse made of aluminum, steel, and fiberglass-reinforced plastic and **steamroll** all opposition." She gave him a wink.
Bob smiled, relieved. "That's a plan." He turned back toward the wall, took a running start and climbed to the other side without a problem. Luckily there were some bushes planted there behind which Bob could hide to **get the lay of the land**. He found himself in the apartment building's inner courtyard, the heart of which was a pool surrounded by palms. Directly adjacent splashed a small fountain. The lush greenery made the courtyard into an oasis of tranquility. Whoever lived here, almost in the middle of the movie city and yet so idyllically, had money, of that Bob was certain.
The pool and the balconies were deserted as far as the Third Detective could tell from his hiding place, but radio music was coming out of one of the open windows and somewhere else the TV was on. Bob struggled out of the bushes and crept around the pool to a large, metal plated wooden door that led into the building. It was standing open. Bob entered a cool

---

that hit home – das saß; **impudence** – Unverschämtheit;
to steamroll – plattwalzen;
to get the lay of the land – die Lage sondieren

hallway with marble tiles that led to the stairway and an elevator. If Bob had correctly interpreted the doorbell panel, Jonathan Thorndike lived on the third floor. He hurried up the stairs and shortly thereafter stood in a hallway where four apartments were **accessible**. On one of the doors hung a nameplate: Jonathan Thorndike, Kimberly Lloyd.

So, the mysterious Mr. Thorndike didn't live here alone. Bob was undecided about what he should do. But before he could develop a plan a shrill, female voice suddenly was heard from the apartment:

"Do you seriously believe I'm buying this, Jim? I saw you! You were standing directly in front of her and suddenly … suddenly … she collapsed! Oh, no, you can tell me what you want. She fell! And there was blood! So much blood! You didn't perhaps kill her, did you, Jim! You didn't perhaps kill her, did you! I … Jim! Jim, why are you looking at me like that? You're **scaring** me! What are you doing? What … Jim! Jim, stop it! I … aaaaaaahhhh! Heeeeeelllppp!"

---

accessible – erreichbar, zugänglich;
to scare s.o. – jmd. erschrecken

Kimberly Lloyd

Bob acted without thinking. There was no more time for a plan. The woman was in danger! Absolutely determined, he reached for the **doorknob**. The door was locked. He **jiggled** it. Then he eventually knocked on it. "Open up!" he shouted. "Open up the door immediately! I'm calling the police!"
Inside it had grown quiet. Was it already too late?
But then, suddenly something **stirred** behind the door. And some seconds later it was opened by a slim woman in a bathrobe. Her long, brown hair was disheveled and she looked at him confused. "For goodness' sake," she said and laughed quietly. "You … weren't eavesdropping perhaps?"
"Where's the guy?" Bob asked **briskly** and pushed past the woman into the apartment. "Did he threaten you? Should I call the police?" The apartment was large and flooded with sunlight. Colorful rugs and pillows lay everywhere on the light parquet floor, there were only a few pieces of furniture. Bob looked left, looked right – and hesitated. No one was there.
The woman came toward him. She grinned. And didn't appear at all as if she had been threatened by someone a few seconds ago. "Can I help you somehow?"
"I … I thought … Didn't you call for help?"
She shook her head and held up a small **stack** of stapled paper. "That was Catherine."

---

doorknob – Türknauf; **to jiggle** – an etwas rütteln;
to stir – sich regen; **briskly** – forsch; **stack** – Stapel

"Catherine?"
"The role that I'm learning the lines for right now. I'm an actress, in fact. Kimberly Lloyd."
"You ... You were only acting that?"
Instead of answering, Kimberly held the screenplay in front of his face. Bob scanned a couple of sentences: And there was blood! So much blood! You didn't perhaps kill her, did you, Jim! The Third Detective sensed his face **flushing**. He would have preferred to **disappear into thin air**. "I ... I ... I'm sorry, Mrs. Lloyd, I didn't know ..."
"Miss Lloyd," she corrected him and then broke out in bell-like laughter. "Don't worry about it. It actually means that I must have acted convincingly, right?"
"Very convincingly," Bob thankfully **grasped at the straw** that could pull him at least a little bit out of the **quagmire of embarrassment**. "Really, that was ... marvelous. Do ... do you perform in the theater?"
"Film. I'll make it big with Catherine. And now to you: Why were you eavesdropping at my door? You don't live here. I've never seen you."
"I ... wasn't eavesdropping. I just was going by."
"Were you visiting someone?"
"Yes."
"Whom?"
Bob **swallowed**. Feverishly he tried to remember a name from

---

to flush – rot werden;
to disappear into thin air – sich in Luft auflösen;
to grasp at a straw – nach einem Strohhalm greifen;
quagmire of embarrassment – Sumpf der Peinlichkeit;
to swallow – schlucken

the doorbell panel. Without success. "I … there wasn't anyone there."
"Who wasn't there?"
Bob **cursed** himself inwardly. Why was he so nervous! His heroic attempt to rescue Kimberly Lloyd had completely **rattled** him. Why was he here? Because of Jonathan Thorndike!
"Well, honestly: I wanted to visit Mr. Thorndike."
Kimberly Lloyd raised her eyebrows in surprise. "Jonathan? He's not here. What do you want from him?"
"That's a private matter," answered Bob and tried to act sheepish – which wasn't difficult for him. "Do you know where I can find him?"
"He's pretty busy at the moment. But maybe I can help you out."
"No, that's unfortunately not possible. I have to speak with him personally. It's really very urgent."
"Is it about the movie?"
"About the … movie?"
"About the movie. Everyone wants to talk to Jonathan about the movie at the moment. Actually, filming begins the day after tomorrow."
"That means I'll likely find him at the studio?" asked Bob. He had thought his question was actually quite brilliant, it almost forced Kimberly to **divulge** Jonathan Thorndike's **whereabouts**. But for some reason Kimberly's facial expression changed drastically. She squinted her eyes suspiciously. "In the studio? Tell me, what was your name?"

---

to curse – (ver-)fluchen; **to rattle** – durcheinanderbringen;
to divulge – preisgeben; **whereabouts** – Aufenthaltsort

"Robert," Bob said quickly and that wasn't a lie.
"Robert. And the rest?"
"Robert ... Miller," answered Bob and hoped that Kimberly had not noticed the slight hesitation.
"Never heard it. How do you know Jonathan?"
"That's not at all important now," said Bob who suddenly had the unpleasant feeling that he had walked into a **trap**. He moved toward the door. "If he's not here, I'll come back later, OK?"
But before Bob could reach the door, Kimberly had already blocked his path. "I think you should stay a little bit, Robert. That is to say, I don't believe a single word." With those words she reached behind herself, shut the apartment door and stuck the key in the pocket of her robe. Then she took out her cellphone and dialed a number. "Hi, Vince. This is Kimberly. Come over for a minute. There's a guy here who wants to make trouble. I'll explain it to you later. Hurry up! See you soon!" With a sweet smile she turned again toward Bob. "Vince is my personal trainer. An **impressive physique**. He'll get you to talk!"

Peter's hand lightly shook when he held it out to the doorknob. He closed his eyes and pressed it downward. The door ... remained closed. Peter sighed. He didn't manage to pick the lock. He had been so sure about it! Disappointed he rattled the door – and suddenly it swung open. A burst of cold air came into them. Behind it lay absolute darkness.
For seconds Peter and Jolene were speechless in surprise.
"It worked!" whispered Jolene.

---

trap – Falle; **impressive physique** – beeindruckende Erscheinung

"Yeah." Peter stuck his head cautiously through the door. For a short moment, he had entertained the hope that it would lead outside into freedom. But the icy wind **decimated** that hope. When his eyes had adjusted to the darkness, his **misgiving** was **affirmed**: Beyond the door was a corridor. A long, dark corridor, five or six meters wide with a **rough concrete floor** onto which a square of light fell where Peter's silhouette was clearly defined. To the left, the corridor ended after a few meters at a windowless wall. To the right, he was soon lost again in darkness. In between, there were **rows** of countless closed steel doors on both sides.

Jolene stuck her head out. "Now what?"

"Now we're getting out of here."

"Getting out of here? But how –"

"The corridor has to end somewhere. And there's also a way out, we just have to find it." Peter took a step out the door. "Come on, Jolene!" Jolene hesitated a brief moment, then she followed him.

To walk along the dark corridor, passing by the white doors right and left was like a vision from a **nightmare** where you run and run without ever reaching your destination. For a split second, Peter considered whether he perhaps was really dreaming. But then a sound pulled him back to reality.

"I heard something!" whispered Jolene, who was standing still just like Peter and listening intently.

"Yeah, I heard it, too. A click."

"Maybe it would be better for us to turn around!"

---

to decimate – zunichte machen; **misgiving** – Befürchtung;
to affirm – bestätigen; **rough concrete floor** – rauer Betonboden;
rows – Reihen; **nightmare** – Albtraum

"Yeah, right!" retorted Peter and had to **pull himself together with all his might** to sound cool and **composed**. "That was probably Justus stuck behind one of these doors. Justus!" Peter's voice reverberated endlessly and sounded so **eerie** that he **got chills down his spine**. Seconds later, he heard a spooky, dull knocking.

"Someone's pounding against the door!"

"There it is!" Peter sighed and started moving again. It didn't take long until they had found the door behind which someone was still banging. Peter kneeled down. There was just enough light to be able to work on the lock. After a minute the Second Detective had picked it. He stood up and yanked open the door.

A young woman was standing in front of him, hardly older than Peter, short and slender and shivering because of the cold. Frightened, she looked from Peter to Jolene and back again, clearly considering whether she was standing across from friend or **foe**.

Peter didn't know who was more surprised – she or he.

"Who … who are you? Where am I? How did I get here? I don't understand anything!"

---

to pull oneself together with all one's might – sich mit aller Kraft zusammenreißen;
composed – gefasst; **eerie** – schaurig;
to have got chills down one's spine – eine Gänsehaut über den Rücken jagen;
foe – Feind

The S.E.L.I.I.P.I.C.W.H.

The doorbell rang. Kimberly Lloyd's smile became a bit sweeter and she pressed the door buzzer.

Bob broke out in a sweat. He had to get out of here! As quickly as possible! The **sinister** Vince would be showing up any second and then it would be too late. But Kimberly Lloyd was still standing **nonplussed** in front of him and didn't once think of moving out of the way, let alone to unlock the door. Of course, Bob could try to forcefully **escape**. But then if he ran into Vince, it would be over. On the other hand, if he remained calm, he at least still had the chance of **weaseling his way out of the whole mess**. Maybe.

Someone knocked.

Kimberly walked backward to the door, unlocked it and opened it without looking. "That was quick, Vince. Come in! This guy **harassed** me. I thought you could maybe teach him a few **manners**."

"I'll gladly try. He's probably earned it. But my name isn't Vince, but Jelena. And I'm here to **collect signatures**. It certainly hasn't escaped you that the elevator in your building is in catastrophic condition. For someone in a wheelchair it is next to impossible to enter without help from strangers. The

---

sinister – ominös; **nonplussed** – ungerührt;
to escape – entkommen, fliehen;
to weasel one's way out of the whole mess – sich geschickt aus der Affäre ziehen;
to harass – belästigen; **manners** – Manieren;
to collect signatures – Unterschriften sammeln

Society for the Elimination of Life-Impeding Injustices for the Physically Impaired Citizens of West Hollywood, abbreviated S.E.L.I.I.P.I.C.W.H., of which I am the chairman and only current member, has taken on the task of **combatting** these scandalous conditions. You can become a member at no cost and in turn receive the society's quarterly newsletter. However, a small **donation** would also assist the society. The Elimination of Life-Impeding Injustices for the Physically Impaired Citizens of West Hollywood impacts everyone, you too."

During her speech Jelena had hardly breathed. Instead, without asking, she had simply rolled bit by bit into the apartment and had pushed the completely dumbfounded Kimberly farther and farther back, until at last she was standing at the other end of the room and was trapped between the balcony door and Jelena. "What, have you gone completely crazy?" she sputtered and slowly **regained her composure**.

"Do I gather from your question that you aren't interested in becoming a member?"

"Certainly not! And now get out of here, you insane cow!"

"OK. Goodbye." Jelena turned and rushed to leave the apartment.

Bob had obviously used the opportunity to disappear. He waited in the hallway for her. "Out of here!" he whispered, grabbed the wheelchair and started running.

"Hey! Stop!" called Kimberly, but Bob had already disappeared around the next corner and steered toward the elevator. One look at the display told him that the elevator had been summoned downstairs.

---

to combat – bekämpfen; **donation** – Spende;
to regain composure – die Fassung wiedergewinnen

"Vince!" whispered Bob. "He's coming up!" He looked around in a panic. It wouldn't have been a problem to take the stairs, but with the wheelchair …

Jelena **tore herself loose** and steered toward a small door directly opposite the elevator. She pushed it open. Behind it lay a small, dark **broom closet** where buckets, vacuum cleaners and cleaning supplies were stored. She pushed her wheelchair in regardless. Brooms and buckets fell over, a bottle of vinegar cleaner toppled from a shelf and narrowly missed her head. "Now, come on already!"

Bob didn't have to be told twice. He jumped into the closet, **ascertained** with one last look at the display that the elevator was already on its way up and closed the door. Darkness immediately enveloped him. Holding his breath, he listened.

The elevator door glided open. Heavy footsteps stepped out into the hallway. Then Kimberly's voice was heard from a distance:

"Vince! Did you catch them?"

"Catch them?" boomed a loud bass. "Who?"

"Well, that guy and his girlfriend in the wheelchair. They must have passed by you!"

"I didn't run into anyone. What's the matter anyway?"

"I don't know. There was this guy. Robert Miller is his name actually. He wanted something from Jonathan. But **something didn't add up** with the kid. I think he wanted to **spy** on me."

"Spy on you? Do you think that somebody heard something?"

---

to tear oneself loose – sich losreißen;
broom closet – Besenkammer; **to ascertain** – sich versichern;
sth. didn't add up – etw. stimmte nicht; **to spy** – ausspionieren

"I have no idea!"
"Where is Jonathan anyway?"
"I don't know! I'm really worried about it. I talked with him on the phone this morning for the last time and he said that something had gone wrong and that he urgently had to go to Lasoma. And that later I probably wouldn't be able to reach him anymore, because his cell doesn't work down there."
"Down there? What did he mean by that?"
"I don't know. I only talked to him **briefly**, he was in a terrible rush."
"And what's he doing at Lasoma?"
"I have no idea."
The voices slowly became more and more **faint**. Bob dared to breathe again. Kimberly's voice could only be heard very quietly: "But this guy, this Robert … if he didn't pass by you – then he must still be here somewhere."
"Where?"
Kimberly was silent. And **Bob's stomach was in knots**.
"If she's not a complete idiot, she'll figure out any minute where we are!" whispered Jelena. "We have to take off!" She kicked Bob forcefully in the back of the knees. Bob lost his balance, **stumbled forward** and fell out of the broom closet into the hallway.
"I heard something!" exclaimed Kimberly. She had just disappeared with Vince around the corner. But now quick footsteps were getting closer. Bob pushed himself up and banged on the elevator button. Infinitely slowly, the door glided open.

---

briefly – kurz; **faint** – entfernt;
Bob's stomach was in knots – Bob rutschte das Herz in die Hose;
to stumble forward – vorwärts stolpern

They slipped into the elevator and Jelena pushed the button for the ground floor.
Kimberly and a two meter tall guy, broad like a wardrobe and with forearms as big as Bob's thighs, ran toward them. The sliding door hadn't even thought of closing. Then, when Vince had almost reached them, it did close. Still, he pounded with his fist against the steel panel, but it was already too late.
"Ciao, Vince!" shouted Bob and the elevator started moving.

The young woman's name was Leah. Finding that out was not in the least bit difficult. For everything else, Peter and Jolene needed considerably longer. Leah was closemouthed. After the relief of not being locked up anymore, she had first wanted to hear the whole story from Jolene and Peter before she spoke a word about herself. In contrast to them, she had woken up half an hour ago completely alone in this room. The rest **disturbingly overlapped** exactly with Peter's and Jolene's experiences: Leah didn't know where she was and how she had gotten here. Quickly she had become panicked. But now in Jolene's and Peter's company, she calmed down astonishingly quickly and soon exuded a cool composure that powerfully impressed the Second Detective.
"It's a very complicated story."
"You can say that again," Jolene agreed.
"What do you have planned now?"
"Justus has to be somewhere in the **vicinity**," answered Peter. "We have to find him and free him! With his help we'll definitely get out of here, I'm absolutely sure of that."

---

disturbingly –beunruhigend; **to overlap** – sich decken mit;
in the vicinity – in der Nähe

Leah **nodded** matter-of-factly. "All right. Let's go!"
After both of the young women had left the room, Peter looked around one more time. It was just as bare and white as in their own prison, the rooms were nearly identical. However, the water pipes on the walls were missing. And, therefore, there was no possibility of hiding a camera.
"Are you coming?" asked Jolene.
Peter turned around and walked back into the corridor. It was time for him to worry about the First Detective.

For half an hour icy silence reigned. Justus walked back and forth in their cold prison, in order to distract himself from the freezing cold, while Shawn had crawled back into his corner and incessantly watched the First Detective. Justus continued as if he didn't notice. But Shawn's **penetrating gaze** from his almost black eyes was nearly physically **palpable**. Justus couldn't concentrate. Shawn completely disrupted his train of thought by his mere presence and his silence. His dark stare seemed to suck all of Justus's thoughts out of his head. Finally, he stood still in frustration and **anger** and turned toward Shawn: "What's up?"
"What's up with what?"
"Why are you staring at me?"
"I'm not staring."
"You're following me with your eyes. Do you think I'm not noticing that?"
"Where else am I supposed to look? There's not much here."
"It's making me nervous. I can't think."

---

to nod – nicken; **penetrating gaze** – bohrender Blick;
palpable – spürbar; **anger** – Wut

"You poor thing. But just in case it hasn't occurred to you yet: Thinking hasn't helped us one bit up 'til now."
"Oh, no?" protested Justus. "And what about Peter? And the camera?"
"Great, Justus, really great! And what does it matter that your **shady buddy** is trapped down here somewhere, too? Nothing at all! We're still locked up. So **stop being so full of yourself**."
"Then you stop lying finally!" hissed Justus and bit his lip. He desperately looked for a way to make what he said less harsh or to **put a different spin on it**. But one look at Shawn's face made it clear to him that Shawn had **smelled a rat**. He knew now that Justus didn't trust him. Still worse: that he entertained a definite suspicion.
"What are you saying?" Shawn asked threateningly.
All that was left for Justus to do was **charge full steam ahead**: "You're keeping something from me. I know it. There's no point denying it."
"I'm keeping something from you," repeated Shawn trying hard to keep his cool. "Are you also going to tell me what that might be and why you think so?"
"Gladly. You just said that we're trapped down here. Down here. Why do you think that we're down somewhere?"
Shawn rolled his eyes. "Because there aren't any windows here, you Superdetective."

---

shady buddy – dubioser Kumpel;
stop being so full of yourself – hör auf, dich wichtig zu machen;
to put a different spin on sth. – etw. abschwächen;
to smell a rat – Lunte riechen;
to charge full steam ahead – die Flucht nach vorne wagen

"And what about the warehouse?" Justus continued determined. "You were talking about a warehouse before. Are you also concluding that from the fact that there are no windows?"

"That was a guess, man!"

"A guess. Shawn, no one would have simply thought of a warehouse. And what was your freaking problem with the camera?"

"What are you even talking about?"

"When I discovered and took apart the camera, you were less than enthusiastic. I would even go so far as to say that you would have preferred it if I hadn't found it. Can you convince me that **I'm delusional** and that I'm only imagining everything, or are you ready to finally tell me the truth?"

Shawn's face went blank, looked at Justus expressionless and didn't **reveal** the **slightest indication** what he was thinking. When he finally answered, his voice was also completely emotionless: "I don't know what you're talking about. A cold, bare room without windows – looks to me like an underground storage possibility for frozen groceries for example. Or something like that. Haven't you noticed the fish smell yet? Fish are laid on ice after they're caught and stored before or after processing. We could be in a **fish cannery**."

Justus stopped himself from agreeing. Shawn was right. The theory was actually plausible. And he could have thought of it himself. But he hadn't. "And what about the camera?"

Shawn smiled thinly. "Just because I'm not a know-it-all like

---

to be delusional – Wahnvorstellungen haben;
to reveal – preisgeben; **slightest indication** – kleinster Anhaltspunkt;
fish cannery – Fischfabrik

you who thinks he has to express all of his discoveries immediately in **stilted words**, doesn't mean that I have something to hide. It just doesn't matter to me, understand. I don't want to run my mouth idiotically and act like I could beam myself through the door by just talking. I just want to get out of here."
"Then we have the same goal. And nevertheless you've **thwarted** every one of my efforts to free us. I –"
Shawn jumped up in a flash. The mask of indifference had crumbled to dust within an instant. Now his face was contorted in fury. "Now listen to me! I've slowly had it with your **blabbering**! It's not helping us, understood! So leave me alone with your **foolish conspiracy theories** once and for all! If you think you can get us out of here, then please do it, instead of blowing hot air! Otherwise, shut up! And don't ever **insinuate** again that I had something to do with that idiotic camera or whatever else! On the contrary: if I find out that you are playing some kind of game and are behind this, then I'll tear you to shreds. Understood?"
While Shawn was yelling at him, he had continued walking toward Justus. Now their faces were only a few centimeters apart. Justus felt his warm breath.
Something clicked. The noise came from the door. Shawn and Justus looked over. Suddenly the door swung open and Peter stuck his head inside. "Hi," he said and **sauntered nonchalantly** into the room. "So, Just? How's it going?"

---

stilted words – gedrechselte Worte; **to thwart** – ausbremsen;
blabbering – Gequatsche;
foolish conspiracy theories – alberne Verschwörungstheorien;
to insinuate – unterstellen;
to saunter nonchalantly – lässig schlendern

Forgotten Past

After Justus had found his voice again, there was no more stopping him. He and Peter **yammered** at each other **incessantly**. Jolene, Shawn and Leah also introduced themselves and reported what had happened. For several minutes, Peter and Justus were so relieved to have found each other that they completely forgot the situation in which they found themselves.

After a while it was Shawn who interrupted the flood of words. "It's great that we're all friends now, but can we finally get out of here?"

Justus refrained from making a biting remark and nodded. "Shawn's right. We can worry about the question of how we got here later. Now we should first try to find an exit." He walked out into the corridor and looked left and right into the darkness.

"How far did you come?" he asked Peter whispering.

"Our prison was back there," answered the Second Detective and pointed to the left. "And Leah's there. We don't know yet what's on the other side."

"Then let's go!" Shawn pushed past both of the detectives and took the lead. Justus let him do it without protesting. Shawn had accused him often enough of being full of himself. This was the opportunity to prove to him that he had been wrong and that for Justus it wasn't always about being the leader at all cost.

---

to yammer – aufeinander einreden; **incessantly** – ohne Pause

The light quickly disappeared behind them. Shortly thereafter, the five were walking through an ice-cold darkness. With every step the light grew weaker. Until Shawn stood still and pushed a switch on the wall. A bluish white flash shot through the darkness, and a second later a fluorescent light lit up on the ceiling. Then a second. And like a flashing, buzzing wave the light continued in both directions along the corridor and illuminated dirty white concrete walls and dull steel doors from which gray paint was peeling off. Justus, Peter and Jolene **stopped in their tracks like deer in the headlights**.
"Turn it off again!" whispered Peter.
"Why?" Shawn replied at a normal volume. "We've hardly seen anything else."
Leah also remained calm. "Do you want to hide in the dark? From whom then? There's no one here."
"But …" Peter fell silent. They were both right, of course. Nevertheless the unsettling feeling remained of suddenly being **on display** and of being at the **mercy** of an unknown power.
The corridor ended after five or six more doors at an approximately three meter wide roll-up door made of scratched aluminum. It was locked as Peter confirmed with a quick look at the mechanism in the floor.
"Can you get it open?" asked Shawn.
"I'm not that familiar with roll-up doors. Besides that, I don't have the correct tool. But I'll attempt it."

---

to stop in one's tracks like deer in the headlights – in der Bewegung verharren wie Kaninchen im Scheinwerferlicht;
on display – auf dem Präsentierteller;
mercy – Gnade

"What about the other doors?" Leah chimed in. "It's very possible that there are more people down here. Maybe they haven't yet woken up or don't dare draw attention to themselves?"
"You're right," said Justus. "It would be **irresponsible** to leave someone behind helpless. We should first check all the other rooms before we take a chance on the roll-up door."
"Before I take a chance on the roll-up door," corrected Peter, but then nodded and looked back into the corridor. "There must be twenty doors on each side. It's going to take a while."
The Second Detective turned toward the first door on the right side and worked on the lock. He was successful very quickly. The room was no different from the three rooms that they had already seen. Door by door he worked through the corridor while Justus, Shawn, Jolene and Leah accompanied him and discussed their situation in more detail.
"We should use the time and ask ourselves why we're here at all," said Justus. "I mean: Why us specifically? There must be some **similarity** between us."
"We're all about the same age," said Jolene. "Well, Peter and you are a couple years younger. And we're from the same area. But other than that … What we do and what we remember we've already discussed. I don't see any similarities."
"Really?" asked Leah. "What are the last images in your memory?"
Justus, Shawn and Jolene reported one after the other about their memories.
"For me it's very similar," said Peter. "I know that we were at the scrapyard. Your aunt wanted something from us. But I

---

irresponsible – unverantwortlich; **similarity** – Gemeinsamkeit

have no idea anymore what it was. The memory … is fading. As if you're not quite sure if you dreamed something or really lived it."

"It's exactly the same for me," said Leah. "I was sitting with my brother in the car. We had gone shopping together. And then … it gets **dimmer** until eventually nothing's there anymore."

"Absolutely nothing more?" Justus **dug deeper**.

"Absolutely nothing more. And for you?"

Justus thought about the image of the ax-shaped island that had whizzed through his head. And there had been something else when he had awoken. A dream. But try as he might he couldn't remember what it had been about. Or if it had meant anything at all. He shook his head. "No, nothing. But at least we can hold onto the fact that the amnesia began for us all at about the same time, namely yesterday afternoon. So, if we were to believe Peter's watch, approximately twenty-four hours ago."

"But how?" asked Jolene. "How can it be that five people completely independent of each other have lost their memory and regained consciousness again here? I mean, are we here because of the memory loss – or did we lose our memory, because we're here? And how is it possible at all – that the memories suddenly stop?"

Justus sighed. "Of course I have no proof, but the longer I think about our **collective** amnesia, the more certain I am of having an explanation for it."

---

dimmer – blasser;
to dig deeper – genauer nachhaken;
collective – gemeinsam

"An explanation?" perplexed, Jolene looked at the others. Leah appeared just as curious as she was, while Shawn eyed the First Detective suspiciously. "What kind of explanation?"
"The whole story reminds me of a case that we were involved with once. We met a couple people, who had likewise lost their memory. In the end, it turned out that they had been administered something: a liquid substance that **robbed** them of their memory."
"Just!" exclaimed Peter appalled. "Of course! Those people were also watched with cameras!" And turning to Jolene, Leah, and Shawn he continued: "A couple of idiots, who had too much time and too much money, found it funny to **bet** on how their test subjects reacted in certain situations. It was people from TV. Just, do you think perhaps … exactly the same thing is happening to us now?"
"I don't think so, Second. It wouldn't make sense, because we're still in an absurd situation, even though we discovered the cameras a while ago. Besides that, there were only cameras in your and in our room. In Leah's and in the others, there weren't any. And not here in the corridor either, I already took a close look around. Don't ask me what it means, but one thing is certain: The case is definitely different from the case in the Valley of Horrors back then, even if I can't yet figure out the **correlations**."
"And what happened with the **victims**?" Leah asked intently. "Did they regain their memory?"

---

to rob – (be-)rauben;
to bet – wetten;
correlations – Zusammenhänge;
victim – Opfer

"No. The hours **encompassing** the **loss of their capacity for remembering** were irretrievably lost. They could sometimes only vaguely remember short scenes that seemed like a dream to them, however. I have to admit, I also have the vague sense that there are some kind of dream images in my head. But I can't get to them. Like how you sometimes know after waking that you had a nightmare without being able to remember what it was exactly. But be that as it may, that substance or a very similar one that someone must have administered to us is the one logical explanation for the situation we find ourselves in. Presumably, the same person who locked us up here."
Thoughtful silence reigned for a while, as Peter switched from the right to the left of the corridor and now moved door by door in the direction of the roll-up door again.
"Well, great," mumbled Jolene finally. "So, someone gave us something. But who? And why? What's it all supposed to mean?"
"What it means?" asked Shawn grimly who had been conspicuously quiet until now. "I can tell you that, Jolene." Without warning Shawn ran at the First Detective, grabbed his **collar** and pushed him forcefully against the wall. "It means that Justus is playing a completely **twisted game**!"

---

to encompass – umfassen;
loss of their capacity for remembering – Verlust ihres Erinnerungsvermögens;
collar – Kragen;
twisted game – übles Spiel

Lasoma

Only after a mile already lay between the yellow VW Beetle and Richmond Road did Bob dare to breathe a sigh of relief and relax somewhat. Up until the last second, he had thought Kimberly and Vince would take up the **chase**. But as **precarious** as the situation had been – Bob and Jelena apparently had not been important enough.

"You haven't said anything yet," Jelena broke the silence.

"About what?"

"About my entrance. Wasn't it great?"

"It was." Bob smiled for the first time since their escape. "It really was. Thank you. How did you know that I needed help?"

"I didn't know. I just had the impression that you were in that apartment much too long. So, I simply rang the doorbell."

"Jelena, I was in there five minutes at the most."

"That's what I said: too long."

"And the crazy woman?"

She laughed. "She **made a racket**, but I didn't care one bit."

Bob sighed. "You rescued me in any case. Vince could've become darn unpleasant. The dumb thing is: I could hardly find anything out. Jonathan Thorndike has something to do with movies and is very busy right now. But if and how Justus and Peter fit in this story – no idea."

"Nevertheless, this Thorndike is our only lead. What did Kimberly tell Vince about where he wanted to go?"

---

chase – Verfolgung; **precarious** – brenzlig;
to make a racket – herumkrakeelen

"To Lasoma," answered Bob. "Whatever that is. I've never heard of it."
"To Lasoma," repeated Jelena thoughtfully, and Bob almost expected her to tug on her bottom lip at any moment. "That doesn't sound like a name, more like an **abbreviation**. What could it stand for?"
Bob had a flash of genius: "La could be L. A. Lost Angeles."
"Good idea! And the rest?"
Instead of continuing to think about the rest of the abbreviation, Bob turned and looked out the side window and drove a little slower.
"What are you looking for?"
"Someone who can help us." Three blocks farther Bob got lucky. He stepped on the brake, parked on the side of the street and got out. "I'll be right back!"
A travel agency with a display window with posters hanging for city tours and sightseeing trips had attracted Bob's attention. The woman at the counter initially didn't know anything about Lasoma, but she had **comprehensive materials** about Los Angeles available and after she had leafed through address books and long lists of city organizations for a while, she discovered something. Bob beamed, thanked her and returned excitedly to the car.
"L.A.S.O.M.A.!" he exclaimed as he got in. "Los Angeles School Of Method Acting. An **acting school**!"
"Wow!" Jelena was impressed. "This Thorndike has something to do with movies, huh? That fits. But exactly what does he

---

abbreviation – Abkürzung;
comprehensive materials – umfangreiches Material;
acting school – Schauspielschule

want at an acting school? And what can all that have to do with a case?"
"We'll figure that out. Off to Lasoma!"

"Hey!" groaned Justus. "Have you gone completely crazy?"
"Shut it, Jonas! As soon as you open your mouth, you lie!"
"Shawn!" pleaded Jolene. "Let him go!"
"What is this?" shouted Leah angrily.
"**Spit it out** now finally, Justus! What's going on here?"
"I don't know!" declared Justus.
"I don't believe a single word from you!"
Suddenly Shawn was grabbed and spun around. Peter had hurried to his friend's rescue. "**Cut it out**!"
For a moment, Shawn seemed to wrestle with whether he should attack Peter, but then he realized that he wouldn't have a chance against the athletic Second Detective and Justus. Breathing heavily, he took a few steps backward and alternately glared angrily at each of them. "You can't tell me any more stories! I know that you're behind it!"
"But Shawn, that's absolute nonsense!" **contradicted** Justus.
"I also think, Shawn, that Justus only tried –," began Jolene, but she was abruptly interrupted by Shawn.
"Justus has tried from the beginning to **dish** us one **fairy tale** after the next! An amnesia **potion**! Don't make me laugh! Completely **by coincidence** our dear prison mate Justus Jonas is the only one who has ever heard of it. Exactly like he coin-

---

spit it out – spucks aus; **cut it out** – hör auf;
to contradict – widersprechen;
to dish a fairy tale – ein Märchen auftischen;
potion – Trank; **by coincidence** – zufällig

cidentally knows Morse code. And his colleague coincidentally knows how to pick locks. Don't you notice anything, Jolene? They are the only ones who knew each other beforehand. The guys want to **put one over on us**! They know exactly what's going on here. Some kind of **underhanded** psychological game, in fact. I didn't trust you from the start, Justus Jonas. But with your strange potion you've just revealed yourself once and for all."

"Shawn, I've already told you a thousand times –"

"I won't believe another single word from you!"

"Just calm down now, Shawn," Peter tried, but it was pointless. Shawn was **livid**.

"You know what? I would beat the truth out of you, but I know that I don't have a chance against both of you. From now on, you can do what you want. I'm not playing your game anymore."

"But –"

Shawn turned around and **abandoned** the group. He stomped down the corridor away from the roll-up door. When he came to the wall, he sat down on the floor and stared gloomily over at the others.

"Honestly, is he **nuts**?" asked Peter.

Justus waved it off. "Let him be, Peter. In a way, I can even understand him. If someone behaved like that toward me, I would also be skeptical. But we can't worry about it. Let's just continue on with our plan!"

Peter turned back to his work. Ten minutes later he had

---

to put one over on somebody – jmd. auf den Arm nehmen; **underhanded** – hinterhältig; **livid** – fuchsteufelswild; **to abandon** – verlassen; **nuts** – verrückt

opened all the doors. Everywhere the same result: The rooms were cold, dark and empty. There were no more prisoners. Only the fish smell that permeated everything had grown even more penetrating. The Second Detective wrinkled his nose. "Tons of fish must have been stored here. It's disgusting!"
"Unfortunately this discovery doesn't help us any," answered Justus and moved toward the roll-up door. "Let's make sure that we get out of here."
"Are you sure that that's a good idea?" asked Leah.
"What do you mean?"
"Well, we still don't know what awaits us behind the door. We're relatively safe here. Behind the roll-up door, however ... anything possible could be lying in wait for us."
Smiling, Justus shook his head. "Whatever's behind this door – it will bring us closer to the answers to our questions. Peter, get to work!"
But it wasn't that easy. As hard as Peter tried, he couldn't pick the lock with his **make-shift** tool. Exhausted, he gave up after fifteen minutes. "Sorry, Justus, but it won't work. This lock is just too complicated for two simple metal clips. We have to try something else."
"Something else?" asked Leah. "Do you want to break the door open? That will never work."
Justus tugged on his bottom lip. "Why not actually? If we used a **lever** ..." He paused, then his face lit up suddenly. "That's an idea! In a couple of rooms I saw narrow, **sturdy heating pipes**! If we somehow tear them out of the wall, then it could work with a lever! Come on, Peter!"

---

make-shift – behelfsmäßig; **lever** – Hebel;
sturdy heating pipes – stabile Heizungsrohre

They hurried from room to room until they finally found a pipe that immediately gave way when Peter hung on it with his whole weight. Excited, they returned with it, pushed it a third of the way into the **gap** under the door and tightly grabbed the other end with both hands.
"On my command, Second. One, two, three!"
Peter and Justus pulled with all their might. Like top athletes, they tried to lift the weight, fighting against it until their faces were red with effort. Justus wanted to give up when the lock suddenly creaked. He called upon his final reserves and tore one last time at the **pole**. There was a cracking sound and already the roll-up door was rattling upward with a deafening noise. The racket reverberated endlessly through the long corridor and back again and it took four or five breaths until the echo had finally died away.
The door was open.

---

gap – Spalt, Lücke; **pole** – Stange

The Direct Way

The Los Angeles School Of Method Acting was located at the edge of West Hollywood on a hill from which you had a clear view of the famous white Hollywood letters. **In conjunction** with the acting school, they seemed to be a promise. Bob found the building itself terrible. It seemed clumsy, cramped and labyrinthine and hurt the eyes with its brown plastic covering on its exterior and tinted window panes.
"Nice," Jelena commented ironically and moved toward the main entrance where a **flurry of activity** was taking place. The students ran hectically in and out, all of them had papers, instruments or athletic bags with them, and on a small patch of grass nearby was a small group that was practicing breathing and **singing scales**.
It didn't look much different inside: **Hustle and bustle** also reigned in the lobby that had been designed with a similarly awful color scheme as the exterior façade. And acting students sat on small benches, tables and seating arrangements and recited quietly to themselves, asked questions of each other or stretched and loosened up their muscles for dance instruction. No one took notice of Bob and Jelena.
"And now what?" asked Jelena.
Bob looked around undecided and then headed toward the **bulletin board**, a huge corkboard, in front of which at least ten students were standing. It took up the entire length of the

---

in conjunction – im Zusammenhang;
flurry of activity – reges Treiben; **to sing scales** – Tonleitern singen;
hustle and bustle – Hektik; **bulletin board** – schwarzes Brett

left wall and was overflowing with small and large, official and less than official looking, slick and brightly colored pieces of paper. Here courses, parties and private study groups were announced, apartments and rooms were sought or advertised, spots in courses traded and used books sold. Bob attempted to get an overview. He had the absurd hope of discovering the name Jonathan Thorndike somewhere in this paper forest. But why would Thorndike have pinned something here on the bulletin board?

"**This stinks**," grumbled Bob. "We found Lasoma, but it's not helping us at all. Even if Jonathan Thorndike is here, we wouldn't recognize him! What are we supposed to do now?"

He looked at Jelena. She was busy. She had just torn down a large piece of paper. Now she was writing on the blank reverse side with a pen. When Bob deciphered what she was writing, he almost panicked.

Looking for Jonathan Thorndike!

"What, are you crazy?" he panted.

"No. You?"

Bob looked around hectically and positioned himself in front of Jelena, so that no one could see the paper. "What's this supposed to be?"

"I'm solving our problem," she answered casually, without looking up from her work.

"Are you going to hang up the paper, or what?"

"What do you think? That I'm going to throw it in the **trash** when it's done?"

"But you can't do that!"

"What, throw it in the trash?"

---

this stinks – so ein Mist; **trash** – Müll

"Hang it up! I mean … I mean …" Bob paused. Suddenly it became clear to him that he didn't even know what he meant.

"Yes?" asked Jelena and grinned. "I can imagine what you mean, Bob. You mean, as a detective you always must **secretly sneak** from A to B and constantly **be on your guard**. **Merely** not to be noticed! Merely not to do anything obvious! But in this case doing the secrecy thing isn't getting us anywhere."

"But what happens if this Thorndike is a **loose cannon** and immediately **goes postal** as soon as he sees the paper?"

"Bob, if you have a better plan: go for it! But I'm afraid we don't have much time to figure something out. Justus and Peter might really be in danger! Believe me, the most direct way is the best here. So, help me hang up this piece of paper!" She pushed the paper into his hand.

Bob stared at it, uncertain. Then he gave himself a kick, looked around, waited long enough until he had the feeling that no one was looking in his direction, and hung up the paper lightning fast, covering up three smaller notices as he did so. Quickly he grabbed Jelena's wheelchair and moved a safe distance away. Then he sat down on an open bench and observed the bulletin board out of the corner of his eyes. "And now?"

"Now let's see if someone reacts to the paper. There are enough people here.. But, for that, we have to get a little bit closer to it." Jelena resolutely gripped her wheelchair tires and looked for a spot that was on the one hand **inconspicuous**, but on

---

to secretly sneak – heimlich schleichen;
to be on your guard – auf der Hut sein; **merely** – bloß;
s.o. is a loose cannon – jmd. ist gemeingefährlich;
to go postal – ausrasten; **inconspicuous** – unverdächtig

the other hand would give her the best view of the notice and even allow her to hear what the people were saying at the bulletin board.
It didn't take long for the first reactions to occur. Most of the students looked at the paper and **smirked**. Others shook their head.
"I admit, I had expected a more meaningful reaction," whispered Jelena after five minutes.
Bob **suppressed a grin**. For the second time today already, Jelena was behaving exactly as Justus normally did. But he preferred to keep that to himself. It wasn't that difficult, because at that moment his attention was distracted by something else: A young couple had stopped in front of the paper.
"Jonathan Thorndike?" a guy with shoulder length hair and a **goatee** asked his girlfriend whose face was half hidden behind a thick head of curls. "He actually was here this morning! If that's really –"
Bob didn't hear anymore, because Jelena was already moving toward both of them. "Hello? Can I speak with you a minute?"

Behind the roll-up door lay a square room as wide as the corridor in which they were standing. The light that fell into it from the corridor was enough to recognize that it was completely empty aside from the wide, double sliding door. The door was made of white-painted metal and had two small windows with a metal grate in the glass. The walls were of a gray, unpainted concrete and completely undecorated.

---

to smirk – schmunzeln;
to suppress a grin – ein Grinsen unterdrücken;
goatee – Ziegenbärtchen

Peter didn't know if he should be disappointed or not. This wasn't the freedom he had hoped for. On the other hand, there was that door …

"A **freight elevator**!" Justus interrupted Peter's thoughts. "This is a freight elevator for transporting large things up and down."

"Fish," commented Peter who had the feeling that the smell had become even more intense after opening the roll-up door. "I'm guessing fish."

"Fish or not, we'll be out soon," Justus said delighted and walked directly to the door. Behind the **panes** was darkness. Justus pressed on the elevator button. Nothing moved. The small light next to the panel remained dark. And as hard as Justus was listening, there was no buzzing or rattling to be heard. He pressed the button a couple more times, but it didn't move. "Or maybe not," he muttered. "This thing seems not to be functioning anymore at all."

"**You don't say**," Peter said bitterly. He rattled the door, testing it. To his amazement it opened with a rusty squeak. Quickly he pushed it completely open and looked into the dark **elevator shaft** where it smelled like machine oil as well as fish. Down below the shaft ended after approximately one and a half meters in a tangle of cables, **steel wire rope** and wheels. Then Peter looked up. About five meters above him the **elevator car** was hanging, blocking the exit. "Hm … climbing up there wouldn't be a problem …"

---

freight elevator – Lastenaufzug; **panes** – Scheiben;
you don't say – was du nicht sagst; **elevator shaft** – Fahrstuhlschacht;
steel wire rope – Drahtseil; **elevator car** – Aufzugskabine

"Climbing up?" Leah interrupted him. "Are you serious? You'll never manage that!"
"Whatever. I'm good at climbing. And it's not that high."
"But if you fall, you'll land in the middle of all the cables and wires!"
"I'm not planning on falling."
"So brave today, Second?" Justus wondered.
"I just want to get out of here, Just. And if I'm seeing it correctly, there's an **emergency exit hatch**. I'll just use it as an emergency entrance hatch instead, pull you up and then we'll clear out of here."
"Do you really think you'll get the hatch open?" asked Jolene hopeful.
"I'll see when I'm up there."
"**I'm on pins and needles**!" said an arrogant voice behind them. The four turned around. Shawn had appeared without anyone having noticed and was leaning casually in the corridor. "Get to it, Peter, climb up!"
Peter frowned. He didn't completely understand what Shawn wanted to tell him. But it didn't matter to him. He reached decisively into the shaft and tested the steel wire rope on which the **counterweight** for the elevator hung. It was **firmly taut**. The oil had made it somewhat slippery, but for a couple of meters it would work. He **gathered momentum** and pulled himself up.

---

emergency exit hatch – Notausstiegsluke;
I'm on pins and needles – Ich bin sehr gespannt;
counterweight – Gegengewicht;
to be firmly taut – straff gespannt sein;
to gather momentum – Schwung holen

Suddenly Leah climbed down into the shaft.
"What are you doing?" Jolene asked, surprised.
"If he won't be persuaded not to climb, I want to at least make sure that nothing happens to him if he does fall. Together we can catch him!"
Justus immediately followed her example. "Good idea, Leah. He'll land much more softly on us than on concrete."
A chuckle was heard from up above. "Yeah, especially on you, Just!" reverberated down into the shaft.
Justus felt himself blush, but the others were nice enough to ignore the Second Detective's remark.
Likewise, Jolene climbed down and looked invitingly at Shawn who was still standing up above. "Come on, Shawn! The more, the better!"
Justus would not have thought that Shawn could be convinced, but he joined them without commenting.
In the meantime, Peter had arrived at the top and looked down for the first time. "It really is high!"
"How does it look?" asked Justus. "Is there really a hatch?"
"Yes. But I don't know how I'm supposed to get it open. I'd need a third hand. Wait a second!" Peter tried to support himself with his feet on the wall to get a more **secure footing**. Suddenly a loud **droning** sounded. A second later the car started moving. There was only a tiny movement, not longer than a **blink**, then it was still again. But that second was enough. Peter was so startled that he **let go of the rope**. His feet slipped. He **plunged** into the **abyss**.

---

secure footing – sicherer Halt; **droning** – Brummen;
blink – Blinzeln; **to let go of a rope** – ein Seil loslassen;
to plunge – abstürzen; **abyss** – Tiefe

Free Fall

The second that he was free falling seemed to happen in slow motion, but simultaneously also incredibly fast. It wasn't possible for him to react. The joke that he had made about Justus's **chubbiness** shot through his head, then something suddenly ripped at his arm. The **jerk** was so forceful that he turned in his fall. He saw Justus's horrified face rushing toward him.
Peter threw the First Detective clear off his feet. Their heads smashed hard against each other. For a brief moment Peter was in a fog. When he came to, Leah and Jolene were kneeling next to him concerned.
"Peter!" cried Jolene. "Is everything OK?"
Difficult question, thought Peter and at first said "Ouch" to be on the safe side.
"Oh, God! You're bleeding!"
"I ... what?" Peter shifted to a more comfortable position and a searing pain shot through his right arm. **Aghast** he looked at a cut approximately ten centimeters long on his forearm from which blood was slowly flowing. He looked up. The sharp ends of a loose steel wire rope that was sticking out in the shaft had slit open his skin. The wound looked bad. Peter became somewhat **dizzy**. "I'm all right," he claimed and looked at Justus. "And how about you?"
"You mean, aside from the fact that you rammed your elbow into the pit of my stomach? And that I lost our small skull-duel? Oh, yeah, just great. But we should climb out of this

---

chubbiness – Pummeligkeit; **jerk** – Ruck;
aghast – entsetzt; **dizzy** – schwindelig

shaft as quickly as possible. Maybe the elevator will start moving again in a second. And downward actually."
Three minutes later they sat leaning against the wall next to the elevator shaft. Justus, Jolene and Leah worriedly examined Peter's arm. It was still bleeding. The Second Detective had become **pale**. With the left he held his forearm tightly, as if he could control the pain that way.
"It doesn't look good at all," murmured Jolene.
"I said it was too dangerous," answered Leah.
"It wouldn't have been dangerous at all, if the elevator car hadn't suddenly moved," said Peter. "Why did it move anyway?"
"Actually there's only one logical explanation for that," said Justus and looked with concern into the shaft.
"And what is it?" Peter wanted to know.
"Someone's up there. Someone's sitting in the elevator or in front of it and someone is eavesdropping on us. He heard that we wanted to escape and set the elevator in motion to scare us off. Successfully. Because it's definitely too risky to attempt it again this way."
"Well, **what a coincidence**," Shawn piped up from the other corner of the room. He had been silent up until now and hadn't even helped Peter climb out of the shaft.
"You stay out of it!" hissed Justus.
"Do you still believe that we're **staging** everything here?" Peter asked angrily. "Do you think I purposely slit open my arm?"

---

pale – bleich; **what a coincidence** – was für ein Zufall;
to stage – inszenieren

"It doesn't matter at all what I believe," Shawn retorted and turned away demonstratively.
Peter forced himself to ignore him. "You really think there's someone up there who's eavesdropping, Just?"
The First Detective nodded.
"But ... but then we must try to establish contact!"
"Establish contact?" Justus laughed. "Whoever's up there already has had a thousand opportunities to get in contact with us. Believe me, Second, we wouldn't get an answer."
"But ... but we can't just keep sitting here, while this guy ..." Peter wanted to stand up, but when he moved his arm, the pain which had leveled off to a dull throbbing came back full force. "Hey!" shouted Peter in the direction of the shaft. "Hey, you! Let us out of here! It's enough, understand? If you free us now, then maybe I'll still think the story is somehow humorous, but slowly I'm really losing my patience!"
No answer came. No one had expected it.
"Now listen to me!" Peter tried again, with substantially more **vigor**. "You're going to be in deep trouble when we get out of here! Not only with me but also with the police!"
"Peter," Justus said reassuringly. "**Save your breath**. That won't help any, believe me."
"But ... but we have to do something!"
The First Detective nodded. "You're right about that. I've been thinking the whole time. But I haven't come up with anything."
In a strange way that sentence **discouraged** Peter more than

---

vigor – Energie; **save your breath** – spar dir die Mühe;
to discourage – entmutigen

anything. If even Justus couldn't think of anything, then the situation was really hopeless.
The First Detective stood up and slowly wandered back and forth. After a short time Jolene joined him. When they were both just **out of earshot** of Peter, Leah and Shawn, Jolene whispered: "We really have to do something, Justus! Peter's wound is still bleeding. Not badly, but … it's not going to stop without something more. We don't have anything to **wrap** it with. If we don't get out of here soon, then …"
Justus nodded. The seriousness of the situation had not escaped him. He was already wracking his brain over how he could help his friend. Worried, he looked over at the Second Detective. Peter had started to **tremble**. Now that he was just sitting in the corner and staring at his bleeding arm, the cold that reigned down here hit him mercilessly. "I know, Jolene. But what are we supposed to do? The shaft is too dangerous. We can't talk with them up there either. What's left then?"
Jolene bit her lip. She seemed to be fighting with herself. She looked at Justus as if she wanted to say something, then she looked away again. She opened her mouth – and said nothing. Then she finally said it, however quietly, so that Justus could hardly understand her mumbled words: "We could pull the emergency brake."
"The emergency brake?"
"Yes. You know."
Justus frowned. He had no idea what Jolene was talking about. "No. What do you mean?"
Jolene looked around and moved another couple of meters

---

to be out of earshot – außer Hörweite sein;
to wrap – (hier) verbinden; **to tremble** – zittern

farther away from Leah and Peter. Hardly audible she whispered without looking at Justus: "We could stop the experiment. It's starting not to be fun anymore. I mean, Peter is hurt! He's bleeding! That definitely wasn't planned."
Justus felt as if he were in a free fall. Suddenly there was only him, Jolene and three words that reverberated in his head. Experiment. Fun. Planned.
This couldn't be. Justus misunderstood something, yeah, of course, that must be it. Jolene was making a joke or something.
"No, this definitely wasn't planned," murmured Justus cautiously. "But how are we supposed to stop the experiment?"
Jolene frowned and answered again in a low voice: "Well, by telling them up there that it's over. That someone is injured. That it was fun, but Peter really **requires medical attention**. He'll understand that, right? I mean, this project can't be that important that he'll just let Peter **bleed to death**. Is his actual name really Peter? Or is that just his character's name? What's the matter with you, Justus? Why are you looking at me so strangely?"

Both of the acting students turned to look at Jelena and Bob.
"Can I speak with you a minute?" Jelena repeated.
"What's up?" asked the boy.
"Do you know this Jonathan Thorndike?"
"Not personally. Although apparently he was here this morning. I unfortunately missed it. He caused quite a **commotion** in any case."

---

to require medical attention – ärztliche Hilfe benötigen;
bleed to death – verbluten; **commotion** – Wirbel

"Commotion?" Bob dug deeper. "How so?"
"Well, he showed up and asked if anyone had time and interest in a film project **on short notice**," the girl answered.
"A film project?"
"Yes," the friend continued. "Something experimental. He explained that two of his actors had **backed out** and he urgently needed **replacements**. Immediately. Of course everyone was **gung-ho**. But you've come too late, the roles are all assigned."
"No, no, it's not about that at all," Jelena brushed it aside. "We're interested for other reasons. Do you know anything more about the project? Did you speak with him?"
"Unfortunately not," the boy answered. "Even though I would have liked to do it. Anyway, Thorndike isn't completely unknown."
"Oh," said Bob. "He's not?"
"Are you trying to say that you don't know him?"
"Um … well …"
"Thorndike is a director. Admittedly he's not that famous, but he has made a couple of great short films."
Bob gave Jelena a meaningful look. Finally that was some information. Even if he didn't know what it meant.
The boy turned to his girlfriend. "Your friend did participate, right?"
She nodded. "Jolene. She's actually just an **acquaintance**. But she told me about it briefly. Thorndike needed someone who is good with theatrical improvisation. And for today, in fact.

---

on short notice – kurzfristig; **to back out** – abspringen, absagen; **replacement** – Ersatz; **to be gung-ho** – Feuer und Flamme sein; **acquaintance** – Bekannte(r)

The whole day. She hardly knew anything about the project herself. The whole thing is very **secretive.**"

Frowning, Jelena and Bob looked at each other. They couldn't **make any rhyme or reason of** this story. Justus and Peter had followed a director who wanted to stage an experimental film? Bob had the distinct feeling that the tip of the iceberg was standing in front of him. But underneath that a completely different story was hidden, about which he had no idea right now. "Do you know where this project was supposed to take place?"

"Hm." The girl thought about it. "At the **harbor** somewhere, I think. In a **storage building** or something."

"Which harbor?" Jelena questioned further. "What kind of building?"

"I think she said she had to go to Long Beach."

"Long Beach?" repeated Bob. "The harbor at Long Beach is huge!"

"I know. But it has to be there somewhere. Don't ask me where exactly. I have no idea."

"Stalker's," the boy said. "Stalker's Fish Company. That's where she was going."

His girlfriend looked at him surprised. "How do you know that?"

"She told me."

"She told you?"

"Yeah."

"But you don't even know Jolene at all."

---

secretive – geheimnisvoll;
to make a rhyme or reason of sth. – sich auf etw. einen Reim machen;
harbor – Hafen; **storage building** – Lagerhalle

"Of course I know her."
She squinted and hissed: "Oh really!"
"Oh really?"
"You're secretly meeting with her!"
The boy was totally flabbergasted. "I … what? No! No, you misunderstood something! I –"
"Oh, cut it out! You can't fool me!"
"Ahem," said Jelena, but no one paid any attention to her. It seemed that she and Bob had **vanished into thin air** for both of them. Questioningly, she looked at Bob. "We should probably go, right?"
Bob nodded. "We're not going to find out more anyway." He continued somewhat louder: "Thank you very much for your help!"
There was no reaction from the couple. Which came as no surprise, because meanwhile they had been **screaming at each other at the top of their lungs**.

---

to vanish into thin air – sich in Luft auflösen;
to scream at somebody at the top of one's lungs – jmd. lauthals anschreien

Thorndike's Project

"Character name?" Justus had planned on **skillfully picking Jolene's brain** without her noticing it. But now he changed his tactics on the spot: He threw all **caution** to the wind. "What are you even talking about?"

"Shhhh!" said Jolene. "There are definitely still cameras or microphones somewhere! We …"

"Cameras?" Justus exclaimed extra loud now so that Peter, Leah and Shawn looked curiously over at them. He didn't want to be alone with Jolene any longer. He needed **witnesses** for the awful things that she was saying.

"What's wrong with you!" hissed Jolene angrily and **dropped her gaze** as if she were talking with the floor.

"Jolene, I …" Justus swallowed. "Are you trying to tell me that we're still being filmed?"

"Well, what do you think! Otherwise he would have gotten us out of here long ago!"

"Who – he?"

"Jonathan Thorndike! The director who's running the project!"

"Jolene." Justus fought for **composure**. "What kind of project?"

"Tell me, are you completely crazy now?" Jolene was furious. Totally different than she had been up until now. Even her

---

to skillfully pick one's brain – jmd. geschickt aushorchen;
caution – Vorsicht; **witness** – Zeuge;
to drop one's gaze – den Blick senken; **composure** – Fassung

voice sounded different. As if she had suddenly **morphed** into an entirely new person. “Do you want to ruin everything?”
“What kind of project?” Justus yelled so loudly that for a few seconds his voice reverberated from the cold concrete walls. Shocked, everyone looked over at him. Jolene stared at him as if he had just revealed a dreadful truth.
“Are you serious? You … mean to say you don’t know anything about the project?”
“About what project, Jolene?”
“About the film project.”
“No. I don’t know anything about the film project.”
“And you’re not trying to put one over on me?”
Justus could hardly **contain his rage**. “Do I look like I am?”
Jolene swallowed. Then she turned around. “Shawn! Shawn, I think we have a problem!”
Contrary to expectation, Shawn started moving immediately. Now Peter became so curious that he struggled to his feet with Leah’s help and joined the group. “What’s the matter here?”
“I’d like to know that too,” Justus said and alternately looked from Jolene to Shawn and back again. Shawn also seemed suddenly wholly different than before. His constant distrustful facial expression, which always seemed to **be chiseled in stone**, had disappeared. Now he appeared really nice, which just plunged Justus further into confusion.
“We have to stop,” Jolene said to Shawn. “Peter is hurt too badly, we can’t be responsible for that anymore.”

---

to morph into – sich verwandeln;
to contain one’s rage – Wut zügeln;
to be chiseled in stone – in Stein gemeißelt sein

Shawn nodded. "That's exactly what I was thinking just now, too."
"Stop what?"
Jolene and Shawn exchanged worried looks.
"Is that supposed to mean you don't know what's going on here?" Shawn asked in disbelief.
"That's what he **claims** anyway," Jolene answered for Justus.
"I don't just claim it. I don't know anything about this project! And Peter doesn't either!"
"Leah?" asked Jolene.
Leah nodded mutely. "I know."
"Well, at least something."
"Now tell us what's really happening already!" Peter demanded angrily.
"What's happening?" asked Shawn. "We find ourselves in the middle of a movie, that's what's happening."
"In a movie? Are you crazy? So like on the holodeck of the Enterprise or what? Everything around me isn't real?"
"No, of course it's real. But we aren't. Jolene, Leah and I – we're actors. **Budding actors**, in any case. I can only assume it about Leah, we haven't met each other before this." He looked at her questioningly.
Leah nodded anew. "I'm in my second year at the acting school."
"Actors? That … that means, you didn't lose your memory at all? And you know where we are and who brought us here?" continued Peter.
"That's right. But I'm gathering from your shock that you don't …"

---

to claim – behaupten; **budding actors** – angehende Schauspieler

"You're gathering darn right!" shouted Peter furious. "We are not actors! We're real!"
"And in contrast to you we don't actually know how we got here," Justus added. Slowly the fog around him began to lift. He was still **confused beyond measure**, but he sensed how he was winning back control over his intellectual faculties. He was slowly comprehending in what kind of situation he actually found himself. Now he still just had to figure out how he had gotten involved in it.
"Listen, we had no idea that you both didn't belong to the team," said Jolene. "We thought you would also be playing your roles. Otherwise, of course we would have already –"
"Jolene," said Justus, "how about you tell us the story from the beginning? And in the **proper order**?"
Jolene nodded. "OK. So: Shawn and I are acting students at the Los Angeles School Of Method Acting. This morning Jonathan Thorndike came into the school **desperately** looking for two actors for a project that started immediately and would last twenty-four hours and for which two people had backed out."
"Who is Jonathan Thorndike?"
"A director. He told us that he wanted to make a film in which the actors were placed in a situation that was completely unknown to them beforehand. Thorndike said there was already a location and everything and the film would take place in a **sealed off** building where cameras had been installed all over so that the actors would be completely alone and no camera people would ruin the acting."

---

confused beyond measure – über alle Maßen verwirrt;
proper order – richtige Reihenfolge; **desperately** – verzweifelt;
sealed off – abgeschlossen

"Thorndike only gave us one direction," continued Shawn. "We were supposed to act as if we had amnesia and couldn't remember what we had done in the last twenty-four hours and how we had gotten to this place. He wanted to leave everything else to our interaction and coincidence. We could develop the role that we wanted to play ourselves. Whether we were more calm or **short-tempered**, more fearful or courageous, it was all our decision. Only one thing was important to him: We should never **abandon** our role!"

Leah nodded. "He stressed that again and again. He said that we would meet other actors in the course of the experiment who likewise would be playing people with amnesia. But no matter what happens, we are supposed to always keep in mind that it is only a movie and continue acting at all costs."

"He was interested in the interaction between the actors who had never seen each other before and who couldn't discuss things **in advance**," Shawn continued. "From the finished material, as much as was usable, he then wanted to **piece together** a movie. Similar to 'Blair Witch Project' back then, you know? Then the director also just sent his actors with a video camera into the woods without them knowing what would await them. I thought that was unbelievably suspenseful and agreed immediately."

"It was the exact same for me," said Leah. "However, I already knew a couple of days ago about the project. That's why Mr. Thorndike stuck me in the single room. He wanted to give you time to familiarize yourselves with the situation."

---

short-tempered – aufbrausend; **to abandon** – verlassen, aufgeben;
in advance – vorher, im Vorfeld;
to piece together – zusammenschneiden

"You … you thought the whole time Justus and I were also actors who were only acting as if they had no idea what was happening to them?" Peter asked in disbelief.
Jolene nodded. "That's right. After all, Mr. Thorndike had informed us of that. Imagine how panicked I was when you suddenly discovered the video camera and immediately smashed it! I thought: What's he doing? That's the camera! But then Thorndike's words came to mind that we shouldn't **interrupt** the acting **under any circumstances**. So I thought that the discovery of the camera was perhaps **on purpose** and was part of the movie. And that there were more cameras that were better hidden and that continued filming us."
"It was like that for me too," said Shawn. "But I decided not to let it show."
"That explains your **odd behavior** after I had discovered the camera," said Justus. "But why did you work against me the entire time instead of helping me?"
"That was all a part of my character. I had thought beforehand that I would play someone who is distrustful of everything and everyone and first believes nothing that anyone tells him. And that's what I pulled off. In every situation. I didn't know that you were really you."
Justus shook his head bewildered. "It's unbelievable. Neither Peter nor I have ever heard of this Jonathan Thorndike! Whatever he told you – he kept quiet about a very important part."

---

to interrupt – unterbrechen;
under any circumstances – unter keinen Umständen;
on purpose – mit Absicht;
odd behavior – komisches Verhalten

Manipulation

Bob and Jelena needed almost an hour on the freeway to reach Long Beach Harbor.
The sun was already low in the sky and bathed the harbor in **golden rays**. The air smelled like oil, salt and fish. A **steady rattle** of tankers, boats and cutters and the squawking of innumerable **sea gulls** wafted to them from the ocean. In contrast to the harbor near Rocky Beach, Long Beach Harbor was truly a **monstrosity** that stretched out over an island, several peninsulas and a confusing system of canals and docks to the size of an **urban district**. Cranes towered above flat warehouses and beyond the **main thoroughfares**, the streets were lined with big and small steel containers with the most diverse labels. In part Bob wasn't sure anymore whether he was still driving on a public street or if he already found himself on a **company's premises**. The farther they drove into the harbor area, the more they lost their sense of direction. They crossed over small and large bridges and parking lots, drove past piers and landing stages, turning their gaze constantly to the left and to the right in the hope of discovering a sign somewhere with the inscription "Stalker's". But after twenty minutes, Bob had to admit that he was hopelessly lost. He stopped.

---

golden rays – goldene Strahlen;
steady rattle – beständiges Knattern; **sea gulls** – Möwen;
monstrosity – Monstrum; **urban district** – Stadtbezirk;
main thoroughfares – Hauptstraßen;
company's premises – Betriebsgelände

"What are you doing?"
"It doesn't make sense, Jelena. **We don't have a clue** where we are. The harbor is huge! How are we ever supposed to find this fish processing plant?"
"Definitely not when we're stopped here," griped Jelena.
"No. But …" Bob trailed off, accelerated again and drove a few more meters. He had discovered a harbor employee who had just gotten out of his truck. "Excuse me!" he called from the open window. "Would you happen to know where Stalker's fish processing plant is?"
The walrus-mustached man in blue overalls seemed to think a moment whether he should react at all or simply continue walking. Finally, he stopped, however, turned toward Bob and grumpily snarled something that Bob didn't understand.
"Pardon me?"
Now the man didn't say anything more at all, but rather pointed down the street with his gloved hand.
"Down there?" Bob attempted to translate the gesture.
The man nodded.
"And then?"
He made the same gesture again, more resolute this time.
"Just straight ahead?"
Again a nod.
"And then I'll find it?"
The third nod. And he was turning around already and going on his way.
The Third Detective looked at Jelena with his eyebrows raised. "Nice man."
Bob could hardly believe it but three minutes later they had

---

we don't have a clue – wir haben keine Ahnung

actually found the fish processing plant. Now that he saw the red and white logo of Stalker's on a gigantic, very new looking sign in front of him, he could remember having eaten this company's **canned fish** a time or two. "Here we are," said Bob and parked in the shadow of a freight container a bit away from the **fencing** that surrounded the company property.

"It doesn't look like a movie is being filmed here right now," said Jelena while she watched the trucks and **fork lifts** that were driving on the property.

"No," Bob agreed. "But I bet that this Jonathan Thorndike is either inside or someone can at least tell us where we'll find him. I'll look around inconspicuously."

Jelena scrutinized him from head to toe. "Inconspicuously? I honestly doubt that in those clothes you won't be conspicuous. Look, the people who are walking around are wearing either blue overalls or white coats."

Bob pursed his lips. "You're absolutely right. But I have an idea!" He got out, opened the trunk and pulled something out that he had had since he had bought the car: a brand-new pair of blue overalls. "I put these in here once, in case I have to do a car repair. Mind you, it's never happened, because when it's broken down, Peter does the repair." He grinned and pulled on the overalls.

"**Snazzy**," Jelena said and **gave him a thumbs-up**. "The perfect **camouflage**."

---

canned fish – Dosenfisch; **fencing** – Umzäunung;
fork lift – Gabelstapler; **snazzy** – todschick;
to give s.o. a thumbs-up – den Daumen in die Höhe recken;
camouflage – Tarnung

"If I'm not back in fifteen minutes –"
"I'll rescue you a second time," Jelena finished the sentence. "One of my easiest exercises! Be careful!"
Bob nodded to her, then he walked in a wide circle toward the fish processing plant. It consisted mainly of a large hall, a parking lot where private cars and company owned trucks stood and a **mooring** for large fish cutters. Behind the hall, a grassy hill with a high **chain-link fence** separated the premises from the neighboring property. Bob decided to get closer from this side.
There was hustle and bustle in the courtyard. Countless workers drove forklifts back and forth between fish cutters, trucks and the plant hall, at least as many walked around busily.
Bob marched as self-confidently as possible onto the premises and headed **single-mindedly** toward the back side of the hall so that anyone would believe he had something urgent to take care of there. But, as it was, no one took notice of him. Finally he stood in front of a row of steel containers that lay close together in the shadow of the hall. The perfect cover. The Third Detective ducked behind them in order to take a closer look at his surroundings.
There wasn't much to see. Some workers walked by, but they were too far away to notice him. There was a steel door that led into the hall. A simple door, not a gate for forklifts or containers. Every couple of minutes someone went in or came out. He could risk it here.
But what then? Jelena was right: a movie was definitely not being filmed here. What would a director be doing here? This

---

mooring – Anlegestelle; **chain-link fence** – Maschendrahtzaun; **single-mindedly** – zielstrebig

was a completely normal fish processing plant. Bob thought and tried to connect all of the information he had in a way that made sense. There was something that Kimberly had said to Vince and that Bob now thought of again: She couldn't talk to Jonathan Thorndike on the phone, since his cellphone didn't work down there. Down there.

"He's somewhere underground!" mumbled the Third Detective. "In a **basement**!"

Of course! Why wouldn't this processing plant have a basement? That was what Bob had to look for!

He waited for a moment when no one was nearby, left his cover and ran toward the back entrance of the plant. He took another deep breath. Then he opened the door.

Justus looked around. For at least the tenth time, his eyes traveled over the walls, the ceiling, the floor. He stared with eyes squinted into the dark corners and shadows of the room, examined the elevator door and the roll-up door. Nothing. Since Jolene, Shawn and Leah had **divulged** the truth, Justus had searched the elevator room and the corridor without finding what had to be here if the story that the three had told really added up. There was only one place that he hadn't yet searched: the elevator shaft.

Unnoticed by the others he **crouched down** and climbed inside. Anxiously he looked at the elevator car that hung only five meters above him. If it were to start moving again, he would only have a few seconds to get himself to safety before it crushed him. On the other hand, as long as he was quiet,

---

basement – Keller; **to divulge** – enthüllen;
to crouch down – in die Hocke gehen

someone would only note his presence in the shaft if there really was a hidden camera there.
He directed his attention to the walls and the floor. There weren't that many possibilities to hide something. And so he was not surprised that he didn't find a camera. But instead he discovered something else:
In the floor near him there was a **small switchboard** affixed to the wall that nearly disappeared in a tangled mass of cables. There were four **trigger switches** that looked like **safety fuses**. Three pointed downward. One pointed upward. Justus frowned. Without knowing the slightest about elevators and their **electrical supply**, he was surprised that all the switches did not point in the same direction. The First Detective didn't think about it for long and **flipped** the fourth switch.
The elevator started moving above him with a metallic squeaking and rumbling. For a heartbeat Justus was so aghast to see the monstrosity weighing tons gliding toward him that he completely froze. Then he activated the switch a second time. Squeaking, the elevator car ground to a halt. Within seconds everyone was standing at the edge of the shaft looking at Justus in shock. "What happened?" Jolene exclaimed. "What are you doing down there?"
"I'm … um … investigating."
"Come out of there or do you want to get crushed!" Jolene quickly reached her hand to him and appreciative, Justus let himself be pulled out of the shaft.
"The elevator car moved again," he explained.

---

small switchboard – kleine Schalttafel;
trigger switch – Kippschalter; **safety fuse** – Sicherung;
electrical supply – Stromversorgung; **to flip** – umlegen

"We heard it," Shawn replied. "Why are you so foolish to climb back down there again?"
"I was looking for something."
"What?" Leah wanted to know.
"A camera."
"And?"
"There isn't one. Just as **few** as anywhere else down here. I searched everywhere really."
Peter frowned. "But that means …"
"That we haven't been watched since we destroyed the cameras in our prisons. This Jonathan Thorndike up there might not even have realized that his project has ended. Because he can't see us anymore, in fact. The question that decides it all is: Why didn't he get us out of here a long time ago already?"
Justus cast a **challenging** look at the group. "Well, does anyone have an idea?"
"Why are you asking us that?" Leah wanted to know.
"Because you know this Thorndike!" Justus exclaimed angrily. "You were in on it from the beginning, in contrast to us! Could it be that **there's more to this whole story** perhaps?"
"What do you mean?"
"I don't know." Furious, Justus squinted his eyes and looked intently at Leah, Shawn and Jolene one after the other. "But one of you knows."
"Pardon me?" asked Jolene.
Even Peter had no idea what Justus was talking about. "Just, what –"

---

few – wenig; **challenging** – herausfordernd;
there is more to this whole story – es steckt mehr hinter dieser ganzen Geschichte

"I didn't discover a camera down there, but instead something else," Justus responded seething. "A **fuse switch**! I **set** the elevator car **in motion** and brought it to a standstill again!"
For a few seconds no one said a word.
"But ..." the Second Detective finally began, " ... but that means that the elevator works!"
"It means much more, Peter: It was operated from down here when you fell, not from up there. And that means thirdly ..." He paused dramatically and looked slowly from Shawn to Jolene to Leah and back again. "That it had to have been one of us."

---

fuse switch – Sicherungsschalter;
to set in motion – in Bewegung setzen

The Traitor

Bob's heart was pounding as he opened the back door to the main hall of the fish processing plant. The **pungent** smell of fish hit him and for a moment took his breath away. The hall was cool and bathed in blue fluorescent light. Nevertheless it stunk as if the delivered fish were lying in the blazing sun at thirty degrees. Quickly Bob got the general idea: He found himself in the back section of the hall where a **string of** overwhelmingly large and loudly pounding **machines** ran at full speed. Dozens of employees stood at **conveyor belts** or drove small trucks through the hall. Some of them were not much older than Bob, probably high school or university students who were earning some extra money in the plant. No one paid attention to the Third Detective. His camouflage suit worked fantastically.
Bob had to find the entrance to the basement. A ramp, a staircase or an elevator. He marched through the factory hall. After he had half-crossed it, he discovered the white double doors of a freight elevator on the left side. There was no one in the vicinity who would want to use it in the near future. With his heart pounding, he approached the elevator and pushed the large, yellow button that was supposed to summon the elevator. But he didn't get that far. For suddenly someone called out behind him: "Hey! What are you doing here?"

---

traitor – Verräter; **pungent** – penetrant, durchdringend;
string of machines – eine Maschinenstraße;
conveyor belts – Fließband

"One of us," repeated Shawn flatly, after Justus had uttered his suspicion. "You don't mean that seriously?"
"I don't have any proof, but the fact is that we were all looking up as Peter climbed up the steel wire rope. No one paid attention to what the others were doing. Without much effort, one of us could have operated the fuse switch for a half second. And that implies that one of us is a traitor who can also answer the following questions: Why can't Peter and I remember anything? How does it fit together with this film project? Why hasn't Thorndike gotten us out of here yet?"
"So there's a traitor," said Shawn. "So far I agree with you. But who says that it has to be one of us three? Why can't you be the one who's leading us around by the nose?"
"You don't have to play the suspicious one, Shawn, that was only part of your role, did you forget already?"
"This time it's not acting, **Mr. Smartie Pants**. I have as little a clue as you do what's going on here. And just as many reasons not to trust you."
"Calm down, guys," said Leah. "It doesn't make sense to **hurl accusations around**. Justus and Shawn are right in any case: **Something's amiss here**. And that's why I'm all for figuring out together who's playing a false game and why. We shouldn't take any further steps before we've figured out who the traitor is." She looked around the circle. Jolene, Shawn and Peter nodded in agreement.
Justus shook his head. "Precisely not that, Leah!"

Mr. Smartie Pants – Herr Schlauberger;
to hurl accusations around – sich Anschuldigungen an den Kopf werfen;
sth.'s amiss here – hier ist etwas faul

"What's that supposed to mean?"
"Don't you understand? We can tell each other what we want, we'll never figure out who is telling the truth and who's lying, because there simply isn't **common ground**. I lost my memory, Peter too, you three didn't. You can **sell me a bill of goods** and I have no chance to **verify** your statements."
"If this story about amnesia is even true," Leah interjected.
"See, that's exactly what I'm talking about," Justus continued. "We can argue for hours, it won't help us. That's why I'll set the elevator car in motion and hope that we'll get to the top."
"So that you can get out of this jam?" Leah said agitated.
"Leah!" Justus shouted angrily. "We're not getting anywhere! If we had worked together from the beginning, we already would have escaped long ago! But something constantly **interfered**! And now you still want to discuss everything, before we make another escape attempt! As important as it is to me to solve this mystery – it won't hinder me from getting out of here! I'm getting the elevator now."
Justus didn't give the others a chance to argue or to hinder him from his plan. More skillful than he had thought himself capable, he climbed into the shaft, bent down to the fuse box, took a deep breath and flipped the switch.

Bob flinched when someone behind him had shouted. He closed his eyes. Now it was over. Someone had discovered him even before he had entered the refrigeration room under the warehouse! What was he supposed to do now? What –

---

common ground – gemeinsame Grundlage;
to sell s.o. a bill of goods – jmd. alles verkaufen;
to verify – für wahr erklären; **to interfere** – dazwischenkommen

"You were supposed to stack the palettes and not fold any boxes!" Bob frowned and turned around. A tall, broad-shouldered man in a white coat had walked directly behind him toward a **temporary worker**, who had probably ended up in the wrong department.
"I'm sorry, Sir, I thought –"
"I don't care what you thought," snarled the man. "Go on, back to the palettes!"
The boy rushed to disappear from his boss's view. And Bob, whose heart was beating like a **jackhammer**, rushed to push the button. Nothing stirred. Nervously rocking up onto his tiptoes Bob waited a while, then he pushed the button again. No success. This was not possible! Why wasn't the darn elevator coming? Impatiently, Bob rattled the double door – which suddenly swung open. The elevator car had been on his floor the whole time!
He looked over his shoulder one last time, and then he slipped into the roomy elevator, shut the door and pushed the button.

The freight elevator started moving. Justus jumped, grabbed Peter's helping hand and wriggled out of the shaft. The elevator glided downward rattling and humming, the elevator floor was already coming into view. Since the elevator car had no door, they could see directly inside.
Justus froze. The elevator wasn't empty. Someone was riding in it, a single person whose legs now came into view. And gradually he saw more of this person. The **slender** legs in light jeans, the white T-shirt and finally the face.

---

temporary worker – Aushilfe; **jackhammer** – Presslufthammer;
slender – schlank

In the Wrong Movie

The man was younger than Justus had expected. He looked a little bit like Shawn: tall, slender, athletic, somewhat **rakish**. The only difference was that everything about him was light: His tousled hair was blond, his skin almost unnaturally pale, his eyes light green. Justus stared at him and for a fraction of a second everything was there again:
A warehouse. A spotlight. A brown, ax-shaped island in a white sea. An important message on a piece of paper that Justus had hidden. Somewhere nearby. All of that shot through his head in fragments of memory like lightning – and disappeared again. The uncomfortable feeling of almost having remembered remained. Confused, Justus tried to force the images into a logical combination before they sank again into his **subconscious**, but it was already too late. The elevator stopped and the young man slowly stepped out. He smiled at them and with a quiet voice said:
"Good day, Justus Jonas and Peter Shaw. Do you remember?"

After the elevator came to a stop and Bob had pushed open the door, he found himself again in a long, brightly lit and above all ice-cold corridor. To the left and right there were a handful of doors with **steam** coming off of their dull, matte surfaces due to the cold. Bob shivered. And immediately his hopes faded. It was so icy that no person would voluntarily

---

rakish – verwegen; **subconscious** – Unterbewusstsein;
steam – Dampf

remain here longer than necessary. It would surprise him if he met someone here. Nevertheless he had to look for a clue.
Bob stepped up to the first door he saw and tried to open it which wasn't at all easy, since there was neither knob nor handle, but rather a lever like the ones he knew from old-fashioned refrigerators. It finally did swing open with a whoosh and a flood of even colder air came toward him in white clouds. With the opening of the door fluorescent lights inside the refrigeration room flickered on automatically. Fish. Freshly caught fish were stored on a bed of ice in styrofoam containers the size of **laundry baskets** that were housed on hundreds of towering steel shelves reaching to the ceiling. Although it was so cold, the **stench** was **wretched**.
Despite its size, the storage room was very well laid out. Bob gathered with one glance that there was really only fish here and no prisoners. Quickly he shut the door again and hurried to the next one. Little by little he entered every room without **encountering** a person. Neither a plant worker nor Justus or Peter. After five minutes, when he was standing in front of the last room, he was so thoroughly cold that his ears, his nose and the tips of his fingers were already **numb**. He could only operate the door lever with great effort. When he opened the door, a man in white overalls with a hood was standing in front of him and was busily writing something on his clip-board. He looked up in surprise.
"Yes?" the man asked, irritated. "What are you doing here?"
"I ... um ... I'm looking for someone."

---

laundry basket – Wäschekorb;
stench – Gestank; **wretched** – erbärmlich;
to encounter – treffen; **numb** – taub

"You're looking for someone? Well, then you can only mean me, because besides me there's no one down here." The man smiled.
"No, I ..." Bob didn't know what he should say. He thought about Jelena. About how she had told him that the direct way was sometimes the best. This man didn't look as if he were up to something. He looked as if he were testing the quality of the fish, nothing more. Bob threw all caution to the wind. "I'm looking for Jonathan Thorndike. Do you happen to be him?"
"Thorndike? Never heard of him."
"Are there ... are there other basement rooms here? Where fish aren't stored?"
The man laughed. "What else is supposed to be stored? We're a fish processing plant here, kid!"
Bob thought it over. Of course it was possible that his **conclusion** was completely false. That Kimberly's **remark** about the **cellphone reception** had absolutely nothing to do with underground rooms. But somehow he had to find a clue!
The man probably had the impression that he had to say something more, since Bob didn't answer. "But you're right of course: Theoretically there could be rooms for palettes and empty boxes as was the case in the old plant. But because of the more highly efficient cooling units in the new hall no one wants to stay longer down here than necessary."
"In the old plant? Which old plant?"
"Well, the one at Dock 15. You probably haven't been working long at Stalker, huh? The company moved just three months ago."

---

conclusion – Schlussfolgerung; **remark** – Bemerkung; **cellphone reception** – Handyempfang

"And … and before this it was at Dock 15?" Bob made sure excitedly.
"Exactly. But the hall was too small and the refrigeration rooms not cold enough, that's why –"
"What happened to the old plant?"
The man shrugged his shoulders, obviously irritated by Bob's sudden interest. "It's empty, I think. That is, wait a second, I think a movie company rented it for several weeks in order to film something there. Why –"
The Third Detective turned on his heel and rushed back to the freight elevator.

Smiling, the young man walked toward Justus and Peter. He knew their names! He knew who they were! Justus, on the other hand, still didn't have a clue and one look at Peter's face told him that it was no different for the Second Detective. But before he could answer the question about whether he remembered, Jolene exclaimed:
"Mr. Thorndike! Finally! I thought you were going to leave us down here forever! Peter is hurt. He has to go to the doctor."
"It's all right, Jolene," mumbled Peter who was much too curious and therefore had completely forgotten his aching arm.
"Are you Jonathan Thorndike?" asked Justus.
The man nodded. "So you do remember then?"
"No. But Leah, Jolene and Shawn told us about you. Not a story which is **completely without holes**, it seems to me."
Thorndike nodded **apologetically**. "I'm sorry. Certainly you have many questions. I … have to explain a few things to you."

---

completely without holes – ganz lückenlos;
apologetically – entschuldigend

"I definitely think so too." Justus crossed his arms in anticipation.
"First of all: Believe me, you were never in danger. Peter's fall was an accident that shouldn't have happened, that I admit. But nevertheless –"
"Nevertheless you **locked us up** here against our will!" Peter said scornfully. He couldn't understand how Thorndike was standing in front of them smiling and could be apologizing mildly!
But Jonathan Thorndike shook his head. "You're mistaken, Peter. But I'll gladly explain it to you."
"That's what I'm asking for," growled the Second Detective and resolved not to believe a word he said.
"It's like this: I'm a director and am working on a film for a large Hollywood studio right now. We rented an abandoned processing plant for filming. But the start of filming was pushed back a few days. So I decided to use this time, **aided by** the space and the equipment available to me, to make an idea reality that I'd had for a long time. An experimental film: Five people wake up in different empty rooms and can't remember how they got there. The others have already explained the concept to you."
"How do you know that?" asked Justus ready to **pounce**.
"Because I was eavesdropping on you. The elevator shaft has **top-notch** acoustics. You can understand every word from the elevator car. I developed the movie idea with a couple of colleagues whom I originally wanted to cast as actors. But I

---

to lock s.o. up – jmd. einschließen;
aided by – mithilfe; **to pounce** – sich auf jmd. stürzen;
top-notch – erstklassig

wasn't completely content with my concept. I wanted the actors to really convincingly act as if they had absolutely no idea what was happening around them. So, at the last second I threw it all out the window: I involved new, unused actors from the acting school: Shawn, Jolene and Leah to whom I gave as little advance information as possible. I only told them the basic idea so that they could act as spontaneous and realistically as possible down here."

"Well and good," Peter said impatiently. "But Justus and I are not actors or have I forgotten that somehow too? How do you explain that?"

Jonathan's constant smile became radiant. "That was the most amazing idea that I've ever had! It came to me only a few days ago. I thought that I'll only get a completely realistic scenario if I have actors in the group who know even less. Who know nothing at all. Not even that they are taking part in a movie. I would have preferred it most if I had taken only those people, but that would've been too dangerous. There had to be some people who knew that everything is only an act. Otherwise panic could have **erupted** among the **participants** of the experiment."

"A panic did erupt!" Peter shouted furious. "At least with me! Experiment! You dragged us here against our will and dosed us with who knows what so that we'd forget everything!"

Jonathan shook his head suavely. "Not against your will." And with that he pulled two folded pieces of paper out of his pocket and handed one to Justus and one to Peter.

The Second Detective **irately** unfolded the piece of paper and

---

to erupt – ausbrechen; **participant** – Teilnehmer;
irately – zornig

read the printed text. And with every word his fury turned more and more into disbelief and amazement.

Herewith I, Peter Shaw, ***of sound mind****, declare that I bear sole responsibility and am appearing completely* ***voluntarily*** *in the film project "Evil Games" by Jonathan Thorndike. For this purpose I will likewise voluntarily, and having sole responsibility,* ***ingest*** *a chemical substance that will* ***erase*** *my memories of the last twenty-four hours. The substance is entirely* ***innocuous****. Studies have found that no noteworthy side effects or long term injury are expected. I most probably will not remember later that I have agreed to this project. I accept this fact. For my appearance in "Evil Games" I'll receive a copy of the completed film. I have no* ***right to a say*** *in the* ***rendering*** *of the movie* ***content****, but I can decide whether I would like to have my name mentioned in the* ***credits****.*

Peter Shaw

---

of sound mind – im Vollbesitz meiner geistigen Kräfte;
voluntarily – freiwillig; **to ingest** – einnehmen;
to erase – (aus-)löschen; **innocuous** – ungefährlich;
right to a say – Mitspracherecht; **rendering** – Umsetzung;
content – Inhalt; **credits** – Abspann

The Secret of the Ax

Bob was completely out of breath when he reached his car. Worried, Jelena looked at him through the open window. "What's wrong? Did something happen?"
"Wrong … company!" gasped Bob and collapsed on the driver's seat, exhausted. "This is the … wrong plant! There's another … one. One that's empty."
"Well, then let's get out of here!" Jelena urged.
Bob nodded. "That's what I'm saying."
But he didn't get to turn the key in the **ignition** because suddenly a black shadow came into his field of vision. He turned his head. A man was standing next to the driver's door. He was tall, was **half-bald** and despite the warm weather was wearing a black coat. He looked at Bob intently, then he knocked on the window.
Bob had no clue who this man was. For a second he considered just driving away and leaving him standing there. But he was probably a harmless **pedestrian** who wanted to ask for directions. Bob rolled down the window.
"Hello. You're Bob Andrews, right?" the man asked and bent down to him.
"I … um … yes."
"Am I happy to meet you! What happened? Did something go wrong? Where is Jonathan?"
Confused, Bob shook his head. "Forgive me, who are you exactly?"

---

ignition – Zündung; **to be half-bald** – eine Halbglatze haben; **pedestrian** – Fußgänger

The man frowned, then laughed. "Right, we have never met. My name is Boyd. William Boyd."

Peter stared at the signature that was his without a doubt. Then he looked over at Justus who was holding in his hands the same document with his name and signature.
The First Detective had already read everything twice and looked with the same disbelief at Peter. "That … that's my signature!"
"Of course it's your signature!" Thorndike laughed. "You could hardly wait yesterday to sign your name!"
"But … but if all of this is really true … how did you happen upon us?"
"You came to me," answered Thorndike. "I put an **ad** in the newspaper. 'In search of young people for a short-term film project.' In response, you called me yesterday. I explained to you that you had to **sacrifice** twenty-four hours for this project and that it had to be the next day. Because the joke was that you must not be able to remember to have read the ad and to have called me. The substance that erased your memory only has a **retroactive effect** on the last twenty-four hours. We met, I explained the details, and you were excited!"
"Excited?" Peter shook his head. "I can't imagine that."
"I can," Justus mumbled quietly.
"Indeed, Justus," said Jonathan and smiled again. "You were all for it. You spoke of a great **challenge** and were of the opinion that despite your amnesia you would get to the bottom of the mystery. You were so convinced that you would be

---

ad – Anzeige; **to sacrifice** – opfern;
retroactive effect – rückwirkender Effekt;
challenge – Herausforderung

successful even without remembering how you got here of being able to solve the mystery. You absolutely wanted to participate. Time was short, so in the end you convinced Peter. The next day, so today, we met here in the warehouse and you signed the papers. I gave you the substance that makes you very tired in the first hour after ingestion and you lay down to sleep in the room. Later I brought in Jolene, Shawn and Leah whom I could only hire at the last second, since I didn't know when someone would answer my ad and really agree. They didn't know that both of you were not actors. Shawn pretended to sleep and waited for you to wake up, while Jolene simply woke Peter up at some point. When you were both awake, you didn't know anything anymore."

"And … and Leah?" asked Justus mechanically, although he wasn't sure that he had already processed all of the information. "Why wasn't she there from the beginning?"

"I wanted to involve Leah later in the action, in order to make the film more interesting," explained Jonathan. "You know, it wasn't planned at all that you would free yourselves. That was supposed to be Leah's job. She was the only one who knew more about the project than the others. But you **turned the tables**. Very well. That made it more exciting for me as the director."

"That means you sat up there somewhere and watched us the whole time with the camera," said Justus.

"Exactly. To get access to the cameras wasn't difficult for me of course. And I purposely didn't hide them very well, so that you would discover them sooner or later. That, too, was part of the plan."

---

to turn the tables – den Spieß herumdrehen

"But … but then the project was over!" said Peter.
"No. Because there are still other cameras. Quite a few."
"There are not," Justus contradicted. "I searched everything. There are no cameras down here."
"Yes, there are. They're hidden so well that you couldn't possibly find them."
"Where?" Justus asked promptly, feeling as if his honor had been damaged. How could these cameras have escaped him as an experienced detective?
Jonathan smiled knowingly, "I can't tell you that unfortunately. It's a **trade secret** so to speak, one of my inventions that I'll get patented soon and expensively sell."
Justus frowned. "What's that supposed to mean? Did you invent white tiles that are transparent on one side and hid the cameras behind them?"
"Something like that. Don't bother, Justus, you won't figure it out. And I really can't tell you, I'm very particular about this."
Justus was **dissatisfied** with that answer, but for the time being left it alone. There were too many other things that he had to process first. That he supposedly had really known twenty-four hours ago what was happening was unbelievable. And yet everything confirmed that Thorndike was telling them the truth. Suddenly the whole story made sense.
"In the end when Peter got hurt, I thought long and hard about whether I should stop "Evil Games". I'm sorry, Peter, I should have done it immediately. My **avarice** for **compelling pictures** and a good story ran away with me. That wasn't fair of me. I hope that you'll forgive me."

---

trade secret – Berufsgeheimnis; **dissatisfied** – unzufrieden; **avarice** – Gier; **compelling pictures** – packende Bilder

"And when Jolene finally told us the truth?" Justus inquired further. "Why didn't you immediately break everything off then?"
"Because it was suddenly clear to me that this surprising **twist** would be excellent in my film. I wanted to keep you in **suspense** a little bit longer. Believe me, I was always watching you. You were never truly in danger."
"Well," mumbled Peter and looked at his arm that had finally stopped bleeding but still throbbed dully. "That depends."
Jonathan nodded. "You're right. I suggest that we get you to the doctor and leave this unpleasant place." He pointed to the elevator.
Peter nodded grimly. "I'm all for that."

Half an hour later, Peter looked at his freshly bandaged arm. After they had ridden the freight elevator up, they found themselves in an old factory hall where some things were already set up for the planned filming that Jonathan Thorndike had talked about. However, they didn't have any time to look around, but rather went right to Thorndike's car that had been parked outside on the abandoned premises. Daylight and the warming rays of sun had done them good and had blown away the last hours of their **subterranean** prison like a bad dream. After a few minutes, it already seemed absolutely unreal that for hours he had actually been in the refrigeration rooms of an abandoned fish processing plant.
In the parking lot they bid Jolene, Shawn and Leah farewell and agreed to meet again at the movie premiere at the latest.

---

twist – Wendung; **suspense** – (An-)Spannung;
subterranean – unterirdisch

After that, Thorndike drove them to a doctor in the vicinity who immediately took care of Peter's injury, which luckily wasn't as bad as it had looked in the meantime. Now it was just the shiny white bandage and the dull ache that confirmed to Peter that the whole thing had really happened.

"I'm still totally confused," he mumbled.

"Because of this small injury?" the doctor asked laughing and clapped him on the shoulder. "Well now, an athletic young man like you surely has experienced worse things already."

Peter waved it off. Of course he hadn't meant the injury but everything else. However, he didn't tell the doctor anything about his experiences, but instead dished him some story about a skateboard accident to **avoid** difficult questions. He stood up from the bed, thanked the doctor and left the practice together with Thorndike and Justus.

"Well," said Thorndike when they were standing on the street. "What a day."

"Definitely," said Peter. "I'm really curious about the movie."

"Not just you, Peter, not just you. I'll get in touch with you as soon as I've viewed the material."

"Truth be told, I'd like to be there when you look at the tapes," Justus said quickly since he was tremendously interested in which perspective it had all been filmed in. Maybe that would shed light on where and how the cameras had been hidden. That he could not solve this mystery to save his life immensely rankled the First Detective.

"I'm sorry, but you signed that you can have no **influence** on the rendering and editing," Thorndike responded with a laugh, climbed into his car and rolled down the window. "So

---

to avoid – vermeiden; **influence** – Einfluss

then, you two, thank you again very much. It was an unforgettable experience. It'll definitely be a great movie."
"Wait a second, you're just going to drive off now?" Justus was surprised.
"Sorry, but I have to. I still have a lot to do today. You know: The next movie awaits. My experiment with you all was just a short **intermezzo**, in fact. I'll call you when there's something new, OK?"
"We don't even have your number!" called Justus. It all went positively too fast for him.
"Yes you do, it's in the newspaper ad. It must be lying around somewhere at your place. Just call me, maybe we'll meet sometime for a Coke or something! 'Til then!" Jonathan started the engine.
"He's in a hurry **all of a sudden**," Peter said.
"Yeah, right? Almost as if he wanted to avoid us asking him more questions. But just wait, I'll figure out how he did it with the cameras. Justus Jonas doesn't give up that quickly."
Jonathan Thorndike stretched his pale arm out of the window again, waved and accelerated.
Justus looked at his arm and froze. While waving, the sleeve of his T-shirt had ridden up. From underneath it a conspicuous **birthmark** came into view. A brown mark that had the approximate shape of an ax.
A brown island in a white sea.
A factory hall. A spotlight. A young man with light blond hair – Thorndike. An important message on a piece of paper that was hidden somewhere close. Very close.

---

intermezzo – Zwischenspiel; **all of a sudden** – plötzlich;
birthmark – Muttermal

"Oh, my God!" whispered Justus.
"What's wrong, Just?" Peter said worried.
"I … I remember!"
"What? You remember? About what?"
"About … about something barely," Justus answered confused. "Actually about nothing at all. It … it's only pictures. There was a hall. The fish processing plant! And a spotlight. And Thorndike. He has this birthmark that looks like an ax, did you see?"
"Um, yeah. And?"
"I wrote something down. A short note, there wasn't any more time. And I hid it."
"You hid a note? When? Where?"
"I don't know when. I only know …" Justus concentrated. He concentrated with all his might. He could not lose this memory again like he had two times already. He had to keep the pictures in his head! The hall, the spotlight, the note. Where was the note? "I know!" he shouted almost hysterically. "I know!" He bent down and took off his right shoe.
"But, Just, what are you doing?"
Justus did not pay any attention to Peter. He had hidden a piece of paper and he had just realized where! He took the gym shoe in his hand and bent it. It was **ancient** and almost **disintegrated** into pieces. There was a **tear** that ran across the heel sole. And a piece of paper was stuck in that tear. Excitedly he pulled it out and unfolded it.
On the paper only six words were written in his handwriting: *Don't believe a word Thorndike says!*

---

ancient – alt; **to disintegrate** – zerfallen;
tear – Riss

Back to the Beginning

"Peter! We have to go back! Immediately!" Justus held the piece of paper in front of the Second Detective's face.
"But … but what does that mean?"
"That means that Jonathan **fed us a line of baloney**! And I knew that he would do that, therefore I hid this note."
"When did you hide the note?"
"Sometime during the period that I can't remember."
"That means now you can remember?"
"No, I can only remember the piece of paper. And the plant hall and a spotlight. I don't know how it all fits together, Peter, I only know that Thorndike lied to us! I hid this paper in my shoe so that I would find it later. The **damaged** sole was probably the most secure place that **occurred** to me quickly, because Thorndike definitely searched our pants pockets. He took all of the papers and stuff!"
"That's right! My **wallet**! My keys! They're still gone! I had completely forgotten that! And you think Thorndike has them?"
"Yes, he does. And he has a whole lot more, the truth that's at the bottom of this whole story, in fact! Come on, Peter, we have to go back to the fish processing plant immediately!"
The Second Detective hadn't quite understood what was wrong, but it was enough for him that Justus was in the know. He was already in the street and hailing the next taxi.

---

to feed s.o. a line of baloney – jmd. einen Haufen Mist erzählen;
damaged – beschädigt; **to occur** – (hier) einfallen;
wallet – Geldbeutel

Luckily both of the detectives could remember where exactly the fish processing plant was located. So it was no problem for them to show the taxi driver the way. Ten minutes later they were in the street in front of the abandoned plant property. The driver named his price.

"Oh, **shoot**!" escaped Peter. "Our wallets!"

"Oh." Even Justus hadn't given it a second's thought that they didn't have any money on them.

"Are you trying to put something over on me?" growled the taxi driver. "You can forget that. If you can't pay –"

"Wait!" exclaimed Justus. "There … there's Bob!"

"Bob?" repeated the driver. "Who's Bob? I don't care. Listen, guys, if you don't immediately –"

"Bob!" shouted Peter, jumped out of the taxi and ran toward the yellow VW that had just come from the other direction and was slowing down. "Bob!"

The VW stopped. Bob got out. "Peter! Peter, thank God! What happened? What … what's the matter? Where were you?"

"Why are you here?" Peter countered just as excitedly.

"That's a long story. Hey, what happened to your arm?"

"Later. Do you have money? We have to pay for the taxi."

"I … what? Money? Yeah, I've got some."

Rushing, Peter paid for the taxi and returned with Justus. He noticed for the first time that there were two more people in Bob's car. A tall, half-bald man had **squished** himself into the backseat and barely had room next to the folded-up wheelchair that belonged to …

"Jelena! Well, slowly but surely I'm not understanding anything at all anymore."

---

shoot – Mist; **to squish** – (hinein-)quetschen

"Me neither," Justus **chimed in**. "But at the moment it's completely secondary. Thorndike's car is up front there. So, he is still here! Come, Colleagues, we have to catch him before he takes off."
"Thorndike?" asked Bob. "Jonathan Thorndike? We're here because of him too. And because of you, of course."
"Well, what a coincidence. Go, hurry up!"
The man, who Bob quickly introduced as William Boyd, climbed out of the car. Then they unfolded the wheel chair and all five of them hurried toward the warehouse hall.
"Justus, Peter, it's me, William Boyd! Don't you remember me?" Mr. Boyd asked on the way.
Peter rolled his eyes. "We know each other? Doesn't surprise me. I've forgotten some things."
When Justus, Peter, Bob and Jelena stormed through the wide open door of the abandoned hall, Jolene and Shawn had already disappeared. Jonathan Thorndike was standing on a **ladder** and screwing something into **steel scaffolding** that hung beneath the ceiling and on which several large spotlights were **mounted**. Justus's **scraps of memory** shot through his head again. There was something about those spotlights ... But before he could think about it, Leah, who was standing next to the ladder and just noticed the unexpected visitors, let out a short scream.
Thorndike looked up and climbed down from the ladder in no time at all. For a long moment his friendly façade disintegrated, but then he had himself under control again. "What

---

to chime in – sich einmischen; **ladder** – Leiter;
steel scaffolding – Stahlgerüst; **to mount** – befestigen;
scraps of memory – Erinnerungsfetzen

… hey, here you are again already. Did you forget something?"
"Indeed," grumbled Peter. "Our wallets."
"Oh yeah, that's right. You gave them to me **for safe keeping**."
"For safe keeping, right," repeated Justus and made it **abundantly** clear that he didn't believe a single word. "I think you still owe us an explanation, Mr. Thorndike."
"More explanations?" Thorndike laughed. "I thought you had enough to think about based on the ones before."
"You can tell someone else your story about the movie. I don't believe you."
"Oh. And why not?"
Justus walked up to Thorndike and held the piece of paper right in front of his face. "That's why not."
"'Don't believe anything Thorndike says.' What is that, Justus?"
"That's a message from the past. From me to me. And to be quite honest, I'm inclined to believe myself more than you."
"And he's absolutely correct in that," a voice behind them suddenly said. William Boyd, who had kept himself hidden, now stepped calmly into the hall. Justus watched as Thorndike grew a little more pale.
"William! What are you doing here?"
"I could ask you the same thing, Jonathan."
"I … well, you can see. I'm getting a couple more small details ready for the start of filming the day after tomorrow."
"I see. You're getting something ready. And Justus and Peter surprised you during these preparations which led you to lock them both up, am I getting that right?"

---

for safe keeping – zur Verwahrung; **abundantly** – (hier) ziemlich

"Mr. Boyd," Justus interjected. "I know we've met each other once before. Unfortunately, I can't remember it at all. Jonathan Thorndike administered a substance to us that has erased the last twenty-four hours of our memory. I would be very appreciative if you could describe your version of the story."
Mr. Boyd nodded. "I'm a movie producer. And therefore Jonathan's boss for the next production, which is supposed to be filmed in part in this hall. But from the beginning Jonathan and I had … differences. He wanted to make a completely different movie from what the studio wanted. He wanted to change the **screen play**, wanted more money and last but not least wanted to **replace** the **lead actress** Carrie Porter in the role of Catherine. But that was absolutely impossible. I consider Mrs. Porter an excellent actress. Besides that, we already had a **contract** with her. Jonathan and I really **butted heads** about that **issue**. In the end, I even entertained the suspicion that Jonathan wanted to sabotage the production in order to **achieve his demands**. That was the point when I called you, the Three Detectives."
"Oh, really?" Justus still had to adjust himself to the fact that everyone else knew more about the past twenty-four hours than he did. "How did you know about us?"
"Well, honestly, I'm a big fan of yours. I've followed your detective career in the press for a few years already and have always wanted to get in touch with you. Yesterday the time

---

screen play – Drehbuch; **to replace** – ersetzen;
lead actress – Hauptdarstellerin; **contract** – Vertrag;
to butt heads – sich in die Haare kriegen;
issue – Punkt; **to achieve one's demands** – Forderungen durchsetzen

had come. I couldn't **shake the feeling** that Jonathan was planning something. So I contracted you to tail him. After all, he didn't know you and for that reason I thought the task wasn't dangerous. But it apparently was. Because you had suddenly disappeared. I was very worried since I couldn't contact you at headquarters or on the cell phone."

"So you were the one who called headquarters **umpteen times** and didn't leave a message on the machine?" Bob said.

"Yes, that was me no doubt. I just wanted to hear if Justus and Peter were back. But they remained missing. I finally drove to the fish processing plant to see if I'd meet Jonathan here. And on the way I passed the new plant and met you, Bob. I had seen your picture in the newspaper."

"And how did you come up with the fish processing plant?" asked Peter. Bob and Jelena then alternately relayed their version of the story. "But I still don't know exactly what it's about," Bob concluded the report.

"About sabotage, I'm assuming," said Mr. Boyd. "Somehow both of you must have found out yesterday during your **surveillance** that Jonathan was planning something unauthorized here in the plant hall. Probably last night. So you came here, observed him ..."

"And then were caught by him," Justus finished the thought and as he did so, turned toward Jonathan Thorndike. "We saw or heard something that we were never supposed to find out about, right? You **nabbed** us and it was clear to you that there was only one way to **get yourself out of this tight spot**:

---

to shake a feeling – ein Gefühl loswerden; **umpteen times** – x-Mal; **surveillance** – Überwachung; **to nab** – erwischen;
to get oneself out of a tight spot – den Kopf aus der Schlinge ziehen

Somehow you had to make sure that we forgot everything that we found out. So you gave us this substance. You couldn't be certain, however, that we wouldn't really be able to remember anything. So you locked us up, installed the cameras and watched how we behaved after we woke up. Whether we remembered or not."

Jonathan Thorndike looked at Justus **expressionless**. For a very long time without saying a word.

"But what?" asked Peter. "What did we see, Justus? What was it that we've forgotten?"

Perplexed, they looked at each other. A **subtle** smile was playing around Thorndike's mouth. "That's really a great story. And a good screenplay could definitely be based on that, right, William? But luckily nothing more. I've told you what really happened. Your speculations are fascinating, but since none of you can remember, they'll likely remain speculations."

Peter **perceived** movement out of the corner of his eye. Beneath the hall's ceiling something was **wobbling**. He looked up and just saw as one of the massive spotlights that was hanging directly above Leah's head broke away from the scaffolding with a **hideous creaking** – and came crashing down!

---

expressionless – ausdruckslos; **subtle** – leicht;
to perceive – wahrnehmen; **to wobble** – wackeln;
hideous creaking – hässliches Quietschen

Crash

The Second Detective yelled out a warning, jumped forward and **shoved** Leah **to the side** at the last second. With a loud crash the spotlight hit the concrete floor and thousands of glass shards sprayed like water droplets through the air.
For seconds, everyone was so startled that no one said a word. And in that silence the memories **arose** like **huge bubbles** in the First Detective's mind. The spotlight! He remembered! "That … that …" he stammered, in order to capture the memory in words before it disappeared again.
"That's happened once before!" Peter interrupted him. "Last night! Right here! And we saw it!"
"You remember?" Justus asked puzzled.
"Yes! Just now! We … we were back there, behind the **concrete pillars** and watched as Mr. Thorndike and Leah did something to the spotlights. One crashed down, probably **inadvertently**, and Thorndike said …"
"He said: 'If this thing lands on Carrie Porter's head then we're rid of her once and for all!'" Justus stared at Jonathan Thorndike. "You were planning to murder the lead actress of your film!"
"So that your girlfriend would get the role!" exclaimed Bob. "Of course! Your girlfriend Kimberly Lloyd! I found out how she's memorized the lines for the role of Catherine!"
Stunned, everyone looked at Jonathan Thorndike. Mr. Boyd

---

to shove to the side – beiseite schubsen; **to arise** – aufsteigen; **huge bubbles** – riesige Blasen; **concrete pillars** – Betonsäulen; **inadvertently** – versehentlich

was eventually the first one who uttered a sound. "Is that really true, Jonathan?"
Thorndike didn't answer. But then Leah piped up. "It's true," she said **remorsefully**.
"Leah!" shouted Thorndike.
"There's no point, Jonathan. The five of them have already figured out almost everything." She turned again to the three detectives, Jelena and Mr. Boyd: "Of course we didn't want to murder Carrie Porter. Just **put her out of commission**, so that Kimberly got the role. You know how **tight** the **film schedule** is. If the lead actress were to **drop out** for a longer period of time, the role would have to be newly assigned. To Kimberly. So we met here in the hall at night and sabotaged the spotlight mounting so that at the right moment … Well, in any case a spotlight already fell yesterday on accident. And both of you saw it. We nabbed you and discovered that you had learned everything. So we had to do something, otherwise we would both be out of a job."
"You both?" asked Justus. "That means you're not an acting student?"
Leah shook her head. "I'm Jonathan's assistant director. And Kimberly's friend. Last night was a nightmare! We had locked you in the basement but didn't know what else we should do with you. Then Jonathan came up with the **ingenious** plan with the amnesia potion. He had heard about this substance

---

remorsefully – zerknirscht;
to put s.o. out of commission – jmd. außer Gefecht setzen;
tight – eng; **film schedule** – Drehplan; **to drop out** – ausfallen;
ingenious – genial

from a friend in the film industry. A couple of TV people had gotten into trouble because of it."

Justus grinned **wryly**. "Yeah. We heard about that. To be specific, these movie people had trouble with us back then: It's a small world."

"Jonathan still had contact with these people in any case and could get the potion. Then we forced you to drink it."

"Shortly before that I must have found an opportunity to inconspicuously write this note and hide it in the sole of my shoe," Justus mumbled thoughtfully. "But what do Jolene and Shawn have to do with this? Both of them really came from the acting school, right?"

Leah nodded. "Jonathan wanted to **hedge his bets**, therefore he went straight to the acting school this morning and involved them and told them the experimental film story. In reality, he only needed two more people who would **converse** with you because that's the only way he could find out if you could remember or not. And with the help of the cameras and the built-in microphones he watched and listened to you."

"Why didn't he just lock us up in the same room and **skip** the stuff with the actors?" Justus wanted to know.

"Because he was afraid that you would be able to help each other **jog your memories**. He absolutely wanted to keep you separated and as long as possible until he could be certain that you had really forgotten everything. But that didn't work since Peter was able to open the door quite quickly."

---

wryly – schief;
to hedge one's bets – auf Nummer sicher gehen;
to converse – sich unterhalten; **to skip** – auslassen;
to jog s.o.'s memories – jmd.'s Gedächtnis nachhelfen

"And then you came into the act," Justus supposed.
"Right. When you both had destroyed the cameras, Jonathan needed another way to continue eavesdropping on you. So he sent me down."
"Jolene and I heard you!" Peter realized. "Just when we had cracked the door, there was a noise. That was you, is that right?"
Leah nodded. "At the last second I was able to hide in the room from which you then 'freed' me. From then on, I was always in the know and additionally I could try to stop you from attempting an escape."
"So you set the elevator in motion and caused my fall!" Peter exclaimed outraged.
Leah nodded conscience-stricken. "Yes. I couldn't let you take off! But then Jolene dropped the bomb and explained about the movie. Jonathan had eavesdropped on everything from the elevator car and realized that he couldn't let the game play out anymore. So he typed up the two **release statements** like mad and falsified your signatures with the help of your stolen IDs. With them he then came down to us and tried to keep the lie about the movie going."
"So there were no more hidden cameras," concluded Justus. "That seemed strange to me right away!"
"Well," said Peter grinning. "Whatever Justus can't explain cannot be, it's that simple."
"Since we've now established the sequence of events," Mr. Boyd chimed in, "it's high time to do my duty: Jonathan, Leah – you're fired. And now I'm calling the police."
As Mr. Boyd took a few steps backward in order to make the

---

release statements – entlastende Verträge

phone call, Justus turned to the director: "I have to say, Mr. Thorndike: **Kudos**! To develop such a good plan in such a short time and to remain flexible the entire time so that the **web of deceit** didn't come **unraveled** – that does **require** a ton of **gumption**. You almost had us."
"But only just almost," Bob added smugly.
"There's still something," Peter said grimly and reached out his hand. "Our things!"
Defeated, Thorndike gave them both back their **possessions**. Peter opened his wallet, checked if anything was missing, and finally pulled out a business card that he triumphantly placed into Thorndike's hand. "In case you ever need detective help after your prison stay."

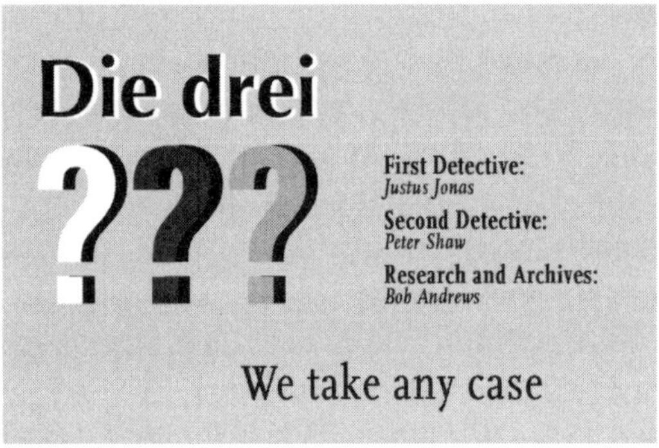

Two days later at sunset, Justus, Peter, Bob, William Boyd and Jelena sat on the veranda of the Jonas's home and ate

---

kudos – Hochachtung; **web of deceit** – Lügengebilde;
to unravel – einstürzen; **to require** – erfordern;
gumption – Grips; **possessions** – Besitztümer

Aunt Mathilda's cherry pie which she had immediately baked a double recipe of out of joy and relief for the return of her nephew safe and sound. Together they discussed once more all the details of the latest adventure they survived.
"What I still haven't quite understood," Bob said smacking his lips, "Why didn't you use my car to drive to the fish processing plant? In the afternoon you were sitting in it in front of Thorndike's apartment, but for the drive to the fish plant you didn't use it anymore. Why?"
"Well," sighed Justus. "Although I can remember the incident with the spotlight again – everything else is still hidden in the fog of amnesia. And it will likely stay that way too. I'm sure that we had a reason not to take the VW. Maybe we were afraid that Thorndike would recognize it. But we'll never know with any certainty."
Peter frowned. "It's a pretty **disquieting** feeling still not to be able to remember, I can tell you. Absolutely anything could have happened in those twenty-four hours! We'll never know!"
"A couple of unanswered questions are good for you," said Jelena and **reaped** an angry look from the First Detective.
"It is going to be pretty difficult to write a report about this case, if you can't tell me what happened," said Bob.
"Does that mean that there are reports for all of your cases?" Mr. Boyd asked with interest.
"Of course," Bob answered not without pride. After all, he had written these reports. "Everything is **meticulously recorded**. Why do you ask?"

---

disquieting – beunruhigend; **to reap** – ernten;
to meticulously record – genau protokollieren

"Well then, as I already said: I've been following your career for a long time already. And not completely without any **ulterior motives**."
Justus's ears perked up. "What do you mean by that?"
"I think you have already experienced many exciting adventures. And if there was an exact record of them, it would be very practical for me of course. For I've considered for a fairly long time whether it would be worth it to make a movie about you."
Peter **choked** and then sprayed pie crumbs over the table. "A movie?"
"Yes. A motion picture. For the movie theater. Maybe even a TV series. Of course I need your **consent** for that. What do you think?"
Die drei ??? looked at each other **dumbstruck**.
Eventually Justus answered with an **impish** grin: "I think if you cast Brad Pitt or Keanu Reeves to play me, then you have my agreement, Mr. Boyd."
The three detectives, Jelena and William Boyd roared with laughter.

---

ulterior motives – Hintergedanken; **to choke** – sich verschlucken; **consent** – Zustimmung; **dumbstruck** – sprachlos; **impish** – verschmitzt